PREACHING THE WORD OF GOD

"In the beginning was the Word, and the Word was with God, and the Word was God.

In him was life; and the life was the light of men."

JOHN 1:1, 4.

Compiled and Edited by
Morgan Phelps Noyes

PRAYERS FOR SERVICES
A Manual for Leaders of Worship

Preaching
THE WORD OF
GOD

BY

Morgan Phelps Noyes

*Minister in the Central Presbyterian Church,
Montclair, New Jersey*

✠

THE SIXTY-SIXTH SERIES OF LYMAN BEECHER LECTURES
ON PREACHING IN YALE UNIVERSITY

NEW YORK
CHARLES SCRIBNER'S SONS
1943

To

MARJORIE CLARKE NOYES

Who helps me to see things visible and invisible.

FOREWORD

THESE lectures are a series of studies in the spirit of the Christian ministry. They do not presume to give technical advice on the making of sermons or on the conduct of a parish. They do not come from an expert in either field. They do come out of the experience of a minister engaged in the everyday duties of a pastorate who has tried to define for himself his approach to some of the problems that confront him in his calling.

For the most part, these lectures are not discussions of the war, but that is not because the war is not a present reality in them. They have been planned and written while the Balkans were being over-run, the battles of Libya held us breathless, the campaigns in Russia staggered our imagination, and the United States turned from an internal war of words to become a partner in struggles on two oceans. Since he was honored with the invitation to deliver these lectures, the lecturer has never been beyond the sound of the guns. Unlike Goethe, who said that he found the cannonading at Jena a not unpleasant sound while he wrote without concern, this lecturer has found the uproar of war a most unpleasant sound, and he cannot discuss preaching in this present world without hearing the guns as an over-tone to all that he says. As a matter of fact, his whole ministry has been within the sound of the guns. He graduated from college in 1914. The first World War broke out that summer. His class held their fifteenth reunion in 1929. That autumn the American illu-

sion of permanent prosperity was ended in the Stock Market
collapse and the beginning of acute depression. He returned
to the campus for his twenty-fifth reunion in 1939. As that
summer ended the second World War began. His whole
ministry, therefore, has been carried on in a world emerging
from war, suffering the consequences of war, and plunging
back into war. He has never been able to think of preaching
except within a period framed by wars. If these lectures do
not deal extensively with the special problems of preaching
in war-time, it is not because the war has been forgotten, but
because the lecturer believes that the basic task of the ministry is the mediation of the truth of God which is man's
deepest need in all contingencies.

These lectures make no apology for leaning heavily upon
the thought of others. This lecturer rejoices in the privilege
of preaching, but he has been only temporarily and by some
mysterious fate which he does not understand a lecturer
about preaching. "Tell us how you interpret the gospel that
you preach," members of the Faculty of the Yale Divinity
School said to him in discussing the task which they had
assigned to him. "What hast thou that thou didst not receive?" he asked himself, and it is what he has received from
others to whom he is profoundly grateful that has gone into
the making of his own convictions concerning the preaching
of the Word of God.

He owes a special debt of gratitude to the people of the
Presbyterian Church of Dobbs Ferry, New York, of the First
Presbyterian Church of Brooklyn, New York, and of the Cen-
tral Presbyterian Church of Montclair, New Jersey, who have
borne with him as their minister and have taught him what
Christian faith can mean in human life. He has grateful

memories of those who attended the Convocation at the
Yale Divinity School in April, 1942, and by their many
courtesies made the delivery of these lectures a pleasant task.
To the Faculty of that School he expresses his deep appreciation of their appointment as Lyman Beecher Lecturer, as
well as his thanks for their kind reception of him as a friend
and temporary colleague. To Dean Luther A. Weigle, and to
Dean Emeritus Charles R. Brown, for their unwearied help-
fulness and constant encouragement, his gratitude knows no
bounds.

                              MORGAN P. NOYES

Montclair, New Jersey.
May 15, 1942.

CONTENTS

Foreword   vii

I.   The Word and The Preacher   1

II.   The Word and The Church   33

III.   The Word and The World   67

IV.   The Word of God for Every Man   103

V.   The Word and The Pastor   135

VI.   The Word and Worship   171

The Lyman Beecher Lectures on Preaching   209

Index   215

"We build our temples of duty and devotion to the Lord our God. We suit them to our growing needs, to the changing demands of new times and seasons; but with our new modes and means of worship, we may set up in them too our fathers' holy things, their true old faith and fervent prayers, the fragrant memory of their good lives, the censers with the incense of their praise still about them. So their dead worship shall give life to ours, so with our Christian prayers shall mingle the noble conservatism that treasures up a Christian past."

PHILLIPS BROOKS (Aetat. 21) 1857

"Let us thank God that we are ministers."

PHILLIPS BROOKS (Aetat. 56) 1891

I

THE WORD AND THE PREACHER

*"Say thou unto them that prophesy out of their own hearts,
Hear ye the word of the Lord."*

EZEKIEL 13:2.

THE WORD AND THE PREACHER

IN a novel in which there is more philosophy than fiction, Mr. H. M. Tomlinson pictures two men as soaring through space and looking down on this pale globe where ingenious creatures have been conquering nature and overcoming the elements and getting the things that they wanted. In spite of their cleverness they have missed some secret that would have made their life a rich and glorious possession. "Man contrived to steal power from the gods, but, the fool that he is, he forgot to bring with it the clue to its right use, and here is Chaos come again!" [1] The two men floating through space look down on a race which is threatened with destruction because while getting the kind of a power it wanted, it has missed something else which it has not always wanted very much—a Word that would give meaning and purpose and dignity to life.

It is the distinctive task and privilege of the Christian minister to be the spokesman of such a Word to the world. The minister is not primarily a philosopher, engaged in the building of a structure of thought roomy enough to house harmoniously his varied knowledge. He is not another essayist, letting his mind play upon the many-sided life of which he is a part. He is not one more commentator, bringing to bear his own background of experience and information upon the swiftly moving events of a tumultuous time. When a man goes into a pulpit to preach, or moves about a com-

[1] *The Snows of Helicon*, p. 93.

3

munity as a minister, he does so because he has been commissioned by the church to be an interpreter of the Word of God to his generation.

That is the minister's privilege, and it is also his central problem. Who is he to speak for God? What assurance can he have that the word he speaks is in any valid sense from God, and is not the expression of his own egotism, or of the mind of the particular segment of society in which he moves, or of ecclesiastical tradition? The popular idea that the only prerequisite for divine guidance is a listening ear is contrary both to the facts of the prophetic tradition and to the facts of contemporary experience. Intuition is undoubtedly one of the avenues to knowledge, when it is yoked with an honest and a humble mind, a high moral character, and a life of varied contacts with sources of knowledge. But any candid examination of intuitive knowledge must conclude that there is an important relationship between what has been stored away in the mind, consciously and unconsciously, and what flashes across the mind in moments of insight. That is not to say that these moments when the truth shines clear are never to be trusted. There are times after a man has wrestled in solitude with his problem and labored and suffered the pains of honest thought, when he comes suddenly into a clearing and sees what he must do and say and be. That is a very different thing from lolling in an easy chair and indulging in daydreams which one mistakes for the revelations of God. One of the minister's main problems is to know when he may speak with confidence that he is giving utterance to the Word of God.

Here we are face to face with the continuing mystery of inspiration, on which the last word will never be said so long as man wonders how the thoughts and convictions by which his life is guided come to him. Without accepting any theory of mechanical inspiration which assumes that God simply dictates ideas to passively receptive minds, either of prophets or poets, it must be said that some minds do penetrate more sharply into reality than others, and that in doing so they are convinced that they are in contact with a superhuman order. In his Queen's Hall lecture on Poetry, John Masefield said:

"It is not possible to speak of poetry without submission to something not understood, that is greater than the perishing self. . . . All the great poets had access to an illumination which came within their beings, as sunlight comes within the sea. . . . The greater poetry is a flowing in of light from the source of all light, from that King from whom comes our knowledge of the kingly, in whose wisdom we advance, under whose majesty we move, and in whose beauty, if we have cared for beauty, we may come to dwell. His ways are the ways of light, and His words are the words of light, vouchsafed to a few great men of light, so that this world may know a little of the wisdom, beauty, and power which are the daily bread in Paradise."[2] Gamaliel Bradford in somewhat similar terms described the experience of the writer: "It is the testimony of all who have made great art and have at all analyzed the process of making it, that something enters in and possesses them far more than mere superficial consciousness or effort. You sit down to your task quite hopeless, discouraged, incapable. Then suddenly, from you know not

[2] *Poetry*, pp. 2, 37-38. Lecture given at the Queen's Hall in London, on Tuesday, October 15, 1931. By permission of The Macmillan Company, publishers.

where, out of the depths of the subconscious, out of the
inherited memory of the ages, the power comes upon you,
and you speak, or appear to speak, with the tongues of
angels." [3]

This may be the despair of the minister who is called upon
to preach one or two sermons every Sunday, and who knows
much more about the halting tongues of men than about
the inspired tongues of angels. He may have rare experiences when his message writes itself and preaches itself. He
is likely to have many more when his message has to be
hammered out by hard work in his study, in the midst of a
week full of demands upon his time and energy which cannot be refused. As he looks back upon his preaching, the
sermons which in the making and the preaching seemed to
be coming to him as the gift of a Spirit beyond himself may
be the very ones of which in retrospect he could say with
least confidence that they had within them the authentic
note of divine authority. The sermons which seem to have
counted most for God may have been the very ones which
were written with most travail of mind and soul, and were
preached with what seemed to the preacher to be a stum-
bling and a feeble tongue. There is only one safe rule for
the preacher in these matters. He can be grateful if he is a
poet whose message sings itself, but he must never rely upon
that gift, if he has it. He must always recognize that he has
the treasure of the gospel in an earthen vessel. There is
always the possibility that he may be mistaken concerning
the details of the will of God, even when he feels most inspired. He can be sure that he will often be mistaken unless,
behind whatever spontaneity of utterance he may possess,

[3] *Life and I*, pp. 109-110.

there is hard study, earnest thought, and sincere prayer. That the gift of tongues has never been the assured reward of clerical indolence is indicated by the fact that even in the fifteenth century a popular form of literature was the "Sleepwell," [4] a compilation of little talks on the gospels ready to be delivered by hard-pressed priests, and guaranteed to insure the Saturday night slumbers of preachers unprepared for their Sunday duties. The most famous, that by John of Werden, entitled *Dormi Secure* is said to have gone through twenty-five editions before 1600. President Charles W. Eliot, referring to his plans for the Harvard Divinity School in his President's Report for 1869-70, said: "The pulpits of the country are not going to be filled by geniuses; if they were, there would be small need of theological schools. They are to be filled by common men of good natural parts, who have been carefully trained for their special work. These men should be scholars by temperament, education, and inveterate habit, else their congregations will drain them dry in a year or two." [5] The truth is that the preacher must come at his message by a double process. He must work laboriously for it, using all the resources of the spiritual and intellectual life in his search for truth. At the same time, he must receive it. After he has mastered facts and principles, certain convictions master him, perhaps in moments of relaxation when he is not at work on them, and these convictions become the framework of the message which he must speak. He at least is sure that they are the Word of God laying hold upon him.

Obviously it is a hazardous thing for any man to attempt

[4] Oscar Hardman, *History of Christian Worship*, p. 164.
[5] Henry James, *Charles W. Eliot*, Vol. I, p. 272.

to speak for God to his generation. History is full of fanaticism and worse which has been the result of honest efforts by honest but foolish or unbalanced men who have honestly believed that the absurdities they uttered were spoken by the divine voice through them. No man can contemplate that story without misgivings when he himself attempts to preach the Word of God. But no man who believes that God does speak through His servants can be deterred by that history if he is convinced that preaching is his vocation, any more than a physician can refuse to practice his profession because there are melancholy pages in the history of medicine which tell the story of quacks, superstitions, and malpractice. The honest preacher will recognize the danger. He will also recognize that he is not merely a lone individual speaking a truth that has come to him and to him only in his solitude. His safety and his truest inspiration lie in his recognition of the twin facts that there have been *historic* revelations of the Word of God, and that there are *contemporary* revelations of the divine will in the larger world of which he is a part. Only as his message has its roots deep in those sources of truth which are wider than the measure of his own mind can he rightfully claim to be a Christian interpreter of the Word which the world needs for its salvation.

II

That is one of the major reasons why the preaching of the Word of God needs to draw its inspirations from the Bible. Preaching which grows out of a study of the Scriptures is not merely following a conventional pattern, as some maintain, nor is it bowing to an ancient superstition, as others believe. It is drawing nourishment from the record of a segment of history through which, by common consent, God has spoken to mankind.

There are, of course, other reasons why the Bible is a fruitful field for the preacher. For one thing, it is interesting. A common complaint against preaching is that it is dull. That is a strange complaint, when one reflects that religion has been at all times and in all places one of the themes with which all men are concerned. There is something wrong when we preachers bore people when we talk about religion. The Bible, when read with imagination and insight, is a fascinating book. Even if the preacher is not himself gifted with the powers of mind and speech which make it possible for him to invest the ordinary affairs of life with new interest, he has at his disposal in the Bible a wide range of literature in which that has been done with genius. For the Bible is human. When preaching is dull, or when preaching fails to be helpful, the chances are that it has gone off into abstractions. The Bible is full of men and women whose problems were not theoretical but very practical. They asked the perennial questions: "What is life for?" "Whence does it derive?" "Whither does it tend?" "How can it be managed?" All thinking people ask those questions when they find that life is not a stream on which one idly drifts, but is an experience which demands intelligence and understanding if it is to yield rich fruits. The men and women of the Bible are people who work for their living, fall in love and establish homes, find their life complicated by the desires of other people that conflict with their own, are puzzled by the chaotic turmoil of their own minds and feelings, are harassed by their relationships with people whom they have wronged or who have wronged them,

are haunted day in and day out by the realization that there
is a spiritual structure to the world, not of their own fashioning, which demands their understanding and obedience. All
human life revolves around such considerations as these in
every age. Preaching which keeps close to the Bible is not
likely to soar off into worlds where the common man has
never been and never wants to be, but will move in the
world where he is and will point him to that world of which
he is perhaps only dimly aware, where his life has its deepest
center.

Moreover, the Bible is inexhaustible. It covers the range
of human needs and divine resources. Every preacher
must frankly face the problem involved in speaking to a
congregation who come looking for help Sunday after Sunday and year after year. A cheap solution is to flee from
one congregation to another when the springs of homiletic
refreshment get low. That is not a real solution at all, but
merely an escape, which may be even more welcome to the
congregations than to the minister. At any rate, it creates
many more problems than it solves for the preacher, and
sometimes results in a very low vitamin content in the fare
which is offered to various congregations in rapid succession.
Every preacher has known during the early days of his ministry the fear that he has said all that he has to say about
the Christian religion, so that the future stretches ahead of
him like a dark, forbidding land through which he must
make his way, he knows not how. That fear indicates that
the essential nature of preaching has not yet been grasped.
Preaching is not talking *about* the Christian religion. It
is talking *to* and talking *with* people who are or ought to be
trying to live the Christian life. That fear also indicates that

a preacher has not yet discovered the resources which are open to him in the Bible.

Those resources are inexhaustible, and the preacher who feeds his mind and his soul on its messages need never have an anxious Monday morning when he wonders what will turn up in the way of a theme for a sermon before the evil days of Friday and Saturday come, and he shall say, I have no pleasure in them. (Homiletic Mr. Micawbers in the pulpit make for Old Scrooges who have forsaken the pew, convinced that what is represented as the Christian spirit is diluted with a large measure of humbug.) The preacher whose preaching draws heavily on the Bible faces the problems of selection and organization of material, so that he may in the course of the year or years help his people into a broad view of the manifold riches of Christ, but he does not fear famine or drought. Moving about among the themes with which the Bible deals, facing the problems with which men and women in the Bible wrestle, considering the different facets of the many-sided faith which the Bible proclaims, living over again the rich life out of which the Bible grew, and in which the Bible's knowledge of God became deep and strong and sure—he has enough and to spare for as long a ministry of preaching as may in the Providence of God be given him.

But when it has been said that the Bible is an inexhaustible source of human interest for the preacher, it must also be said that the main reason for the preaching of the Bible does not lie in that realm at all. The Bible must be preached because through the Bible God speaks to men. For most of us it is not possible to think of the Bible as having been dictated by the divine voice to human recorders who were merely automatic receptionists for the message. The message of the Bible gives every evidence of having come through active minds that were reflecting on the meaning of the strange and dramatic experiences through which they passed. What the Bible has to say about life and about God grew out of the struggles of honest and sensitive men as they faced the wonders and the horrors, the beauty and the slime, the heroism and the sin that go to make up life. And yet God was there, somehow involved in it all, revealing Himself to those with insight enough and purity of heart enough to understand that basic fact. For most of us it is not possible to think of the period of history between the time of Abraham and that of the Seer on Patmos as the only epoch in which God revealed Himself to men. Surely there is a self-disclosure of God in every human apprehension of truth and in every moral advance made by men. The search for truth and goodness, wherever they take place, are the human response to an order of life that is superhuman. God is not only the end of the search. He is the Initiator of the search and the Companion of the searcher, revealing Himself in proportion to the capacity of the searcher to receive the revelation. We do not find truth half so much as truth finds us. Pascal was right when he represented God as saying, "Thou couldst not have sought me if thou hadst not already found me." God has not left Himself without a witness in any age or in any nation. But Hebrew history in one millennium did produce men through whom God could speak in a unique way, and through the Bible in which that message is recorded, God still speaks to men.

In the expansive days at the turn of the century, it was the fashion in theology to think of God as Immanent in the evo-

lutionary process, present in man's thoughts and aspirations
and best efforts, the urge to a higher life of which no man
could be totally unaware. It is unfair to the prevailing liberal-
ism of that day to say that it represented a belief in automatic
and inevitable progress. A study of the preaching in out-
standing liberal pulpits will show that they were in constant
protest against the escalator view of life. But when over-
emphasized the doctrine of the Immanence of God did sometimes lead to so close an identification of divine activity with
the highest expressions of human genius as to make God
hardly distinguishable from the sum total of human virtues.
The Bible became in the hands of some interpreters hardly
more than a sociological document recording some interesting phases of man's development. Since cataclysmic events
have rudely shattered the optimistic outlook of the Victorian
era, it has become the fashion in some theological circles to
go to the other extreme and to concentrate attention exclusively upon the Transcendence of God. God is the Wholly
Other, we are told, who cannot be known in any wise in the
achievements of this world, but who breaks through into this
world in special revelations of the Reality in which He exists
beyond this world. What He reveals is not a power to make
this world better, it is said, but a Heart which forgives those
who are caught in the meshes of a sinful world from which
they can be extricated only by a grace which makes them, at
the same time that they are caught in the toils of sin, dwellers
in another world which is outside history and unrelated to
space and time. The Bible, say some of those who concentrate on the Transcendence of God, is valuable not for its
literature, or for its history, or for its moral teaching, or for
its religion, but because "in the Bible, the strange new world

of God has broken into this world of space and time." [6]
These theologians do not say that the Bible is the Word of
God, or even that the Bible contains the Word of God, but
that it bears witness to the Word which was spoken with
absolute, not relative, authority to men whose capacity to
receive and record was not absolute but relative. The Word
which comes to us through the Bible, they say, is an eschato-
logical Word, promising not development or intensification
of this present life, but an utterly new life of forgiveness and
redemption, forgiveness being interpreted as a new status,
with faint if any emphasis upon moral renewal as a con-
comitant of forgiveness. Fortunately most adherents of this
theology are better than their creeds. While they preach
the helplessness of man they prove themselves anything but
helpless in combating wrongs and in working for righteousness. If carried out rigorously to its logical conclusions, however, this view of the Bible does tend to remove it from a
position of influence on contemporary life.

And yet, through all our interpretations and misinterpreta-
tions of the Book, God does speak to our day and to us as
individuals through the Bible. He speaks to us through the
progressive revelation of Himself which the Bible records
(and in spite of all the considerations urged against it, that
term "progressive revelation" is still the best description of
the method by which God speaks through the Book). He
speaks to us through passages that find us at our deepest
level, challenge us, comfort us, haunt us, persuade us, mould
us. He speaks to us through men, who sin shamefully, sin
stupidly, and sin steadily, and yet are obviously always dealing with One greater than themselves, who will not leave

[6] John McConnachie, *The Barthian Theology*, p. 95 ff.

them in their sins, but strives with them for their redemption by a pursuing, forgiving, empowering Love. He speaks to us through a church, which emerges out of older religious institutions (and it is a weak faith which discredits the divine origin of the church because of that emergence!), a church which creates the literature of the New Testament, and launches the Christian movement of which we are a part. The Bible which we are called to preach is not merely a humanistic document, although it is human. Its central message is a gospel which is "not after man." [7] Neither is it exclusively an other-worldly proclamation, breaking into this world from another world but with no message for this world save that of a mysterious forgiveness which leaves man morally unchanged. As God is both within His universe and beyond it, involved in its affairs and yet greater than them, so the Bible comes out of human life with the Word of the super-human God becoming articulate in it. Its message is curiously mingled with the ignorance and mistakes of the centuries in which it grew. And yet the Bible is infinitely greater than its limitations because through its pages God proclaims Himself to us a loving Father, lays upon us His commandment to love one another, and reveals Himself with fulness in the Cross of Christ. How can we preach the Word of God, if our preaching does not draw deep from the wells of the Bible? How can we be confident that we have the Word of God to preach, unless our message is rooted in the historic revelation which comes to us through this Book?

III

Of course, the supreme authority for our preaching is the Christ whom the Fourth Gospel calls "the Word made

[7] Galatians 1:11.

flesh." There has been endless argument as to the sense in which the Word of God comes to us in Jesus. To the makers of the historic creeds it was primarily through the birth, death, and resurrection of Jesus that God spoke to mankind. There are those today to whom everything else in the record concerning Jesus is incidental. As a reaction against such an exclusively dogmatic approach to Jesus, we have been through a period when the great doctrines concerning Jesus were pretty well forgotten, ignored, or repudiated, and attention was centered on what he was, what he said, and what he did. The truth is that neither approach is complete without the other. If Jesus had revealed a character like that of Iago, had spoken like Hitler, and had done the kinds of things that most of us do, his origin, sacrifice, and destiny would have made very little difference to us. It is because of the kind of life he lived that we want to know the deeper meaning of his life. On the other hand, our faith that he came from God, died for God, and lives with God throws a revealing light upon everything that we see in him, hear from him, and do with him. For if his life and teachings reveal God to us, then they lay an authoritative obligation upon us which it is our supreme duty and our highest privilege to fulfill.

But can we know what this Word is which comes to us through the life and the teaching, the death and resurrection of Jesus? We sometimes talk about "following Jesus" as though it were as simple as walking down a well-lighted street behind a friend who is in full view. But it is not so simple, as everyone has discovered who has honestly tried to be a follower of Jesus. Say what you will, the first century was not the twentieth century, and Nazareth was not New York or

London. The basic human problems of faith and life are the same in every age and in every place, but the detailed terms in which we confront these problems are not the same as those which Jesus confronted. Jesus lived in a world which was familiar with fear and greed and sensuality and sorrow, just as our world is. He did not face the intricate relationships of organized labor and organized capital as we face them, or the deadly assaults upon the mind which modern methods for the control of information and the dissemination of misinformation make possible. His world was not threatened with the mechanization of life, as ours is. Poverty it knew, but poverty in the midst of plenty was not its problem, nor did it know, at least in their modern dimensions, the frictions which have arisen as improved communications have made the world a physical neighborhood without spiritual neighborliness. Not only do we face external problems which Jesus did not face, but we look out upon those problems from an inner world which is different also. We think different thoughts. We have a mental picture of the world in which we live, of its size and shape, of the physical laws by which it is governed, of the extent to which man can control the physical world and of the techniques by which he can do so, utterly different from the mental picture held by Jesus and his age.

We cannot solve our problems by trying to reproduce the details of his life in the midst of our changed conditions. We cannot find in the record of his teaching a pat saying that will be the key to every riddle that confronts us. The whole temper of his teaching is opposed to the legalistic method of solving problems, and the casual way in which he scattered his seed on all kinds of soil indicates that he did not think of himself as the codifier of a set of moral laws which were to be the final word on the vexed questions of divorce, the use of physical force, or the giving of alms. Even the popular formula "What would Jesus do?" is an over-simplified approach to many a problem that confronts us today. In most cases it begs the question by assuming that we know what Jesus would do if he confronted our problems with our knowledge when that is just what we do not know. We can only imagine, and our imagination may be colored by our own pet theories and prejudices and perhaps by our misconceptions of him. It is not a simple matter to be a follower of Jesus, and no honest preaching will so picture it.

Nevertheless it remains true that the Word of God comes to us as nowhere else in Christ. It is not a Word which relieves us of the painful necessity of thinking out for ourselves its implications as they affect disputed ethical questions of our time. Since that is so, there will inevitably be differences of opinion among modern disciples of Christ as to what their duty is in various emergencies, and the maintenance of Christian fellowship will demand a large measure of mutual respect across lines of difference. But all the records about Jesus combine to give us an unmistakable impression of the *kind of person he was and of the kind of faith by which he lived.* Christianity at its simplest believes that this kind of life and this kind of faith are revelations to us of what God wants all men to be and to have. The message of the Christian preacher must always include an honest attempt to relate that revelation of God's will for mankind to the aspects of contemporary life where mankind is confused or wilfully chooses a lower standard.

The preacher must be on his guard lest he deceive himself

at this point. Because he proclaims Christ as the Way, the Truth, and the Life, he may assume that he himself walks undeviatingly in that Way, has received that Truth in its fulness, and is completely identified with that Life. Honest preaching must keep it clearly in mind that we who commend Christ to others are more like Peter who followed afar off than like John who lay on his Master's bosom. More than that, we must be utterly frank in stating what are the ethical possibilities or probabilities as far as we can see them. Recognizing that within the Providence of God moral miracles do happen, still the stubborn fact remains that those to whom we preach will not in all likelihood become completely Christlike tomorrow or the next day or within the span of their earthly lives. Growth is one of the aspects of the spiritual life, and it is no service to people to lead them to expect a state of arrested development, even on the plane of perfection. The popular accusation that American Christianity is "perfectionist" is wide of the mark, for the last thing which any considerable group of American Christians suspect is that they have attained the perfect life. But sometimes our American preaching does seem to imply that the perfect life is possible for human beings and is just around the corner if we would only turn the right corner.

How shall the preacher deal with this ethical gap between human life as it is, and what we know about the life of Christ? It is no solution of the preacher's problem to interpret the Word that comes to us in Christ as a counsel of perfection—a glorious ideal which it is helpful to contemplate but which cannot be closely related to our life. Neither is it any answer to human need to explain the gospel as the product of a fore-shortened world view, which would have been valid had the apocalyptic expectations of Jesus and his contemporaries been verified by subsequent history, as they were not. Nor is it fair to the record or to a morally muddled world to throw away the ethical import of the New Testament altogether, and simply cling to the doctrines which the ages of faith have built upon the New Testament record. Honest preaching must frankly recognize the disparity between our life and everything that we know about the matchless life which Jesus lived. It must recognize clearly that so long as we are human there will be a moral gulf between Christ and us. We must seek no refuge from those plain facts. But we must never grow content with the width of that gulf. We must never cease struggling to close up the moral gap between his life and ours. We must never give up the attempt to be as nearly like him as we can. We must do everything in our power to enthrone his spirit in our common life. The kind of life he lived and the faith by which he lived are standards by which our life must be continually tested, and they are also the goals toward which we must keep climbing. The preacher of the Word of God must see to it that people keep hearing the Word that was made flesh in Christ.

IV

God has also spoken to mankind through the history of the Christian church, and the preacher of the Word must make sure that his message grows out of that great tradition and is congruous with it. God's dealings with mankind have not been confined to the restricted channel of one institution, even so significant an institution as the church of Christ. But surely in the development of a fellowship in Christ which began with a handful of humble folk in an upper room and has spread like light around the world, there is a Word which has a peculiar meaning for the world. The preacher must view the history of the church in its broad sweep and in its large outlines if he is to proclaim the manifold grace of God as the church has experienced it. He cannot confine himself to one isolated age, even so crucial a period as the Apostolic Age, if he is to keep his ear open to all that God has said to His world through His church. What the church believed and how the church worked while the memory of the earthly ministry of Christ was still fresh is important to a degree that can hardly be exaggerated. But the fact that a particular interpretation of truth or a particular form of church government was approved by the apostolic church does not close the door forever on the possibility that some other interpretation may be truer or that some other mode of organization may be more useful.

In recent years it has come to be assumed in certain circles that the period of the Reformers was the time when God spoke the final word on many matters having to do with man's salvation. What Luther or Calvin or Zwingli taught has been invested with a new authority in the minds of many who have gone through the bitterness of disillusionment over the inconclusiveness of modern thought and the wreckage of modern civilization. Certainly the Reformation was one of those times when, in the heat of a great struggle for freedom, some men saw with new clarity the crucial character of the gospel. But it was not a time when God spoke His last word to men. John Robinson spoke for all ages when he wrote in the seventeenth century that God has more light to break forth from His Word. We can humbly believe that God is at work in His church even at the present time, and that it is the whole story of the church from its slender beginnings to its hopes for the future which is the background of the preacher's message.

It is the story of the church as well as of the churches which constitutes the preacher's heritage. Of necessity he belongs to one branch of the Christian church, but he also belongs to the whole church, the spiritual fellowship of Christian people which is greater than any of the forms in which the church is organized. The whole church has given him his heritage of doctrine, as it has tried in different ages and in different thought forms to state its beliefs. It has given him his treasury of devotional literature, in the liturgies and forms for worship which have grown up first in the undivided church and later in the many divisions which have made up the church universal. It has given him the roster of the saints, men and women of faith in every age, some of them canonized by ecclesiastical action, more of them unrecognized by any official sanctification, but men and women whose Christian character has been the richest fruit of the Christian movement. They are the final evidence of the validity of the Christian gospel. No preacher can forget them or forget what God has said through them if his message is to be true to the Christian tradition at its best. No preacher is ever simply an isolated individual hazarding personal opinions on important matters of life and faith and destiny. He is the preacher of a gospel which has been at work through nearly two thousand years of Christian history, and his message for today grows out of the rich soil of the church's ancient and contemporary life.

V

But it is not only in the Scriptures and in history that the preacher finds authority for his preaching. The distinctive genius of the Christian ministry lies in the fact that the minister is both preacher and pastor. This is one of the practical elements in the ministry which differentiates the function of the Christian minister from that of the priest in other religions. The message of the Christian minister grows both out of the historic records of his faith, and also out of a day to day sharing of the varied life of the people to whom he preaches. The Canon Law [8] of the early Middle Ages restricted the right to preach to regularly ordained priests and deacons who had "the care of souls." The later Middle Ages made numerous exceptions to this rule so that the mediaeval counterparts of our modern professors in theological seminaries and Board secretaries might also have parish pulpits open to them on suitable occasions. This broader rule was the wiser, but the older restriction was based on something more than caprice. Every good sermon is in a sense a conversation between the preacher and individual people with whom he stands in a special relationship by reason of his installation as their pastor. The authority with which he speaks derives not nearly so much from the laying on of hands as it does from what knowledge he acquires of their needs and problems and aspirations. It was said of Jesus that "he spoke with authority and not as the scribes." The scribes were adepts in the discussion of the records, but they did not know what was in man or the spiritual needs of the particular men who confronted them. Jesus' authority

[8] Charles Smyth, *The Art of Preaching*, p. 4.

came directly from God who had commissioned him for his task, but it also came from his intimate knowledge of the men and women to whom he spoke. Common people who were all at sea about their faith in God heard him gladly because they sensed in him an understanding heart, and so they were led by him into an assured faith which was life and power to them. No minister can hope for such authority, but neither can he hope for any authority as a preacher which does not include as an integral element a deep understanding of the life of the particular men and women to whom week by week he ministers. As Thoreau related all the problems of the universe to Concord, so he must see and help his people to see not only their own parochial concerns as matters of concern to God, but also the needs of God's world as the concerns of individuals in the local congregation. Preaching which is not merely the fruitless expression of personal opinions but which makes for better and stronger life is preaching which comes out of a faithful, intelligent, and sympathetic pastorate. God speaks a Word to the preacher through the particular needs of the individuals whom he serves as pastor.

VI

God also speaks an authoritative Word through the needs of the wider world in which preacher and people together live their life. In the needs of that larger world the preacher hears the voice of God laying His demands upon those who are devoted to His service. The message of his preaching, if it is to be in any sense the proclamation of the Word of God, must fit into these needs and help to meet them. Of course, as a preacher, he sees these needs through the windows of his parish. He is not primarily a theoretical economist or a politician. He is the minister of a particular congregation. He knows that nothing human is alien to his own congregation. Poverty in city and country, slavery in Africa, racial injustices throughout America, neglected children near by or far away, war laying waste the whole world—these things are part of the life of the people of his church. It is his task to make his people feel that the needs of the world are their needs, and to help them find ways in which they may work for God where the wants of His children are most bitter. Dr. George A. Gordon wrote of Joseph Bellamy who held a pastorate in Connecticut when most of the state was not suburban but rural: "He was a Connecticut pastor, in many ways isolated from the great world of learning; yet in his isolation he annexed the fortunes of the race to his parish, and fixed it in a large view of the universe." [9] It is the privilege of every minister to open such windows for his congregation. He can do so only if he hears the Voice of God in the bitter needs of the world.

VII

The passing of the authority of the pulpit is a favorite subject for lament among some ecclesiastics. The obvious reply is that the authority of the pulpit has not in any proper sense passed away at all. For the authority of the pulpit is not something which is conferred by the official action of church bodies. All the bishops and all the presbyteries in Christendom can lay hands on a man and put him in a pulpit, and he will still speak without authority unless what he has to say carries an inherent authority by reason of its transparent

[9] *Humanism in New England Theology*, p. 71.

truth. Truth is always authoritative. Professor Alfred North Whitehead has suggested that in philosophical writing "the whole effort should be to display the self-evidence of basic truths, concerning the nature of things and their connection. . . . Philosophy is either self-evident, or it is not philosophy. . . . The aim of philosophy is sheer disclosure." [10] Whatever may be the task of the philosopher, surely it is the aim of the preacher to disclose truth. Unless he can express the truth about God in terms that carry conviction, no authority based merely on his status as a minister can be of more than transitory significance. People will not listen to him simply because he speaks from a pulpit if what he has to say is manifestly false or trivial. Even if they do listen because he happens to be entertaining, his message will carry no authority to their minds and consciences. It is good for the preacher that this is so. It is a great gain that pompous pronouncements by preachers no longer carry weight. A minister can have as much authority as the truth of his message deserves —no more. That is all the authority that any minister who is concerned about his mission rather than his prestige wants. In his best moments he prays that he may never be believed or followed except when he is speaking the Word of God.

VIII

A minister is not likely to be a preacher of the Word of God unless that is his highest ambition. There are other ambitions, even in the ministry, which rob preaching of its God-given authority. It is two hundred years since William Law in his *Serious Call to a Devout and Holy Life* said some

[10] *Modes of Thought,* pp. 66-7.

caustic things, which would be called "progressive" if voiced today, about the competitive spirit in education:

"The first temper that we try to awaken in children is pride. . . . We stir them to action from principles of strife and ambition, from glory, envy, and a desire of distinction, that they may excel others and shine in the eyes of the world. . . . And when we have taught them to scorn to be outdone by any, to bear no rival, to thirst after every instance of applause, to be content with nothing but the highest distinctions, then we begin to take comfort in them, and promise the world some mighty things from youths of such a glorious spirit. If children are intended for holy orders, we set before them some eminent orator, whose fine preaching has made him the admiration of the age, and carried him through all the dignities and preferments of the Church. We encourage them to have these honours in their eye, and to expect the reward of their studies from them. . . . And after all this, we complain of the effects of pride; we wonder to see grown men actuated and governed by ambition, envy, scorn, and a desire of glory—not considering that they were all the time of their youth called upon to all their action and industry upon the same principles." [11] Lord Tweedsmuir revealed a different kind of distinction in his moving tribute to his father, a life-long preacher of the Word in a Scottish slum:

"He was wholly without ambition. He did not know the meaning of class-consciousness; he would have stood confidently before kings, and was quite incapable of deferring to anybody except the very old and the very poor. He was not,

[11] *Serious Call to a Devout and Holy Life*, pp. 364-5.

I suppose, the conventional saint, for he was not overmuch interested in his own soul. But he was something of the apostle, and, if it be virtue to diffuse a healing grace and to lighten the load of all who cross your path, then he was the best man I have ever known." [12] One knows that through such a man the Word of God was preached, and that like his Master, he spoke with authority.

IX

A minister is not likely to be a preacher of the Word of God unless he himself is convinced that the Word committed to him is the Word of salvation for a lost world. Thomas DeQuincey described a minister under whose influence he was thrown in his youth, as one of a class "who understand by religion simply a respectable code of ethics—leaning for support upon some great mysteries dimly traced in the background, and commemorated in certain great church festivals. . . . As a preacher, Mr. H. was sincere, but not earnest. He was a good and conscientious man; and he made a high valuation of the pulpit as an organ of civilization for cooperating with books; but it was impossible for any man, starting from the low ground of themes so unimpassioned and so desultory as the benefits of industry, the danger from bad companions, the importance of setting a good example, or the value of perseverance—to pump up any persistent stream of earnestness either in himself or in his auditors." [13] While under the doleful influence of this un-

[12] John Buchan, *Pilgrim's Way*, p. 251.
[13] Thomas DeQuincey, *Confessions of an Opium Eater*, Everyman Edition, p. 28.

inspired preacher, DeQuincey ran across Richard Baxter's famous confession:

> "I preached, as never sure to preach again;
> And as a dying man to dying men."

"This couplet," he wrote, "which seemed to me equally for weight and for splendour like molten gold, laid bare another aspect of the Catholic Church; revealed it as a Church militant and crusading." [14] No man can preach at all today without the knowledge that he is preaching to a lost world. No man is likely to preach the gospel of Christ without reading on the faces of his hearers their conviction that this is the Word of God unto salvation.

Let the preacher speak from that conviction, and all the techniques of sermonizing and the changing fashions in theology are incidental. Simon Patrick, who had a sharp pen when dealing with the eccentricities of the Puritans, complained that during the days of the Commonwealth in England:

"If any Fellow did but light upon some new and pretty Fancy in Religion, or perhaps some swelling words of Vanity; presently he is set up for a Preacher, and cryed up himself for a man that had made some new discovery. And such was the confidence of these men, both in inventing strange language, and proclaiming their great Discoveries every where, that the poor people were persuaded, the Nation never knew what Communion with God meant till this time." . . . But all this signified nothing more than that "the people were much in love with new-minted Words, in

[14] *Ibid.*, pp. 31-2.

which they thought there were great mysteries concealed." [15]
Ola Elizabeth Winslow says that people came away from
Whitefield's sermons talking about "the great Mr. Whitefield" but that they came away from hearing Jonathan Edwards at Enfield asking, "What must I do to be saved?" [16]
Insofar as that is true, it would seem fair to conclude that
through a theology which few of us would accept today,
Jonathan Edwards was what every Christian minister aspires
to be, a preacher of the Word of God.

X

It cannot be said too often that the Word of God is a
word of hope. It is a word of judgment, to be sure, and no
message from a Christian pulpit is true to the gospel which
does not proclaim the Lord who stands over against His
world with a plumb-line in His hand, trying it. It is not the
function of the preacher to make light of the hurt of God's
people, to soothe his hearers with pleasant assurances that
everything will come out all right, or to cry "Peace, peace,"
when there is no peace. But it is the mission of the preacher
to assure his hearers that it is the God and Father of Jesus
Christ who is the Judge of all men. That means that a God
of Love who bears a Cross in His heart is the God under
whose judgment the world stands. All analogies between the
judgments of God and the judgments of an ordinary police
court are wide of the mark. They belong in different realms
altogether. No interpretation of the justice of God which is
incompatible with the love of God is credible. No senti-

[15] Charles Smyth, *The Art of Preaching*, pp. 143-4.
[16] *Jonathan Edwards*, p. 228.

mental interpretation of the love of God which does violence
to the justice of God is either credible or desirable. But the
fundamental affirmation of the gospel that there is an Eternal
Love who will not let men go is a Word of hope. It means
that there is at work in human affairs a Creative Will for
Good that is more than the sum total of human wills, and
a Beneficent Power that is more than the power of man.
History is in His keeping, although with the perilous gift of
freedom in human hands the fulfilment of His purposes
may be long delayed. The Christian gospel can never view
that delay, with all the spiritual suffering and loss which it
entails, as anything but tragic, both for man and God. But
the Christian view is not limited by the narrow horizon of
human history. When the foundations for hope in current
events seem insecure, the Christian faith still stands on the
Psalmist's affirmation, "From everlasting to everlasting,
Thou art God," and although the human mind cannot comprehend the meaning of "everlasting," the human mind can
apprehend the fact that the Eternal God is our hope, not
only for eternity, but for years to come.

II

THE WORD AND THE CHURCH

". . . *For his body's sake, which is the church:*
Whereof I am made a minister . . . to fulfil the word
of God."

COLOSSIANS 1:24-25.

THE WORD AND THE CHURCH

A FEW years ago it was popularly said that there was a growing interest in Christianity, but at the same time a growing indifference to the church. There were many who hoped that it might be possible to discover a way of having a disembodied religion which would mediate spiritual vitality to the individual and be a healing, cleansing, creative influence in society, but which would be untrammelled by anything savoring of organization. That hope is now generally recognized to have been an illusion. It was contrary to the nature of religion, which always in some sense presupposes a community. It was contrary to the history of Christianity, which has been from the beginning inextricably interwoven with the history of the church. They make a large assumption who insist that Christianity is the church, but not so large as those who claim that Christianity can exist without a church. History, at least, has no record of Christianity in a world where there was no Christian church. The hope that there could be such a disembodied Christian spirit transforming the world failed to take account of our actual need, which includes our need for a fellowship from which we can derive an enriching tradition, in which we can find illumination and support, and through which we can work cooperatively for Christian purposes. One could almost say that the dream of a churchless Christianity was contrary to the Christian faith, which is directed toward a God whom His children can address as "Our

35

Father." At any rate, there has come a shift of interest. Much of the new interest is due to a deepening understanding of what the church is. It has come home to our generation with a new emphasis that there is a Word which God speaks through the church.

It is always unfortunately true that we humans take our greatest treasures for granted until we have lost them, or are in danger of losing them. The threats to the existence of the church, and the particular quarters from which these threats came, have led many people to re-examine the history and the contemporary status of the Christian church. They have discovered that there is truth in many of the criticisms of the church which have been the stock in trade of those who have been loudest and most persistent in crying the church down, although the criticisms have lost much of the sheen of novelty through continual use. The church is divided, and many of its divisions are meaningless today. The church does continue to tithe mint, anise, and cummin, and to forget the weightier matters of the law, justice, and mercy, and faith. (That criticism of organized religion, by the way, was originally voiced by One who laid down his life to bring men into a deeper fellowship with God, a fact often forgotten by modern critics who find in the ethical limitations of organized religion a pretext for having nothing whatsoever to do with any kind of religion.) The church has become an institution, and an institution involves such dreary aspects as budgets, programs, committees, and business meetings which were probably unknown to twelve disciples engaged in an itinerant mission with their Lord, although even the Twelve had a treasurer who proved unworthy of his post. Sometimes the institution does crush the life of the spirit in the church, although the remedy lies along the line of deepening the spirit, rather than in wrecking the institution. (Perhaps a modest amount of wreckage would not be intolerable. Even in London it is said that the destruction of churches has not been all loss from the standpoint of religion, although an irreparable loss from the standpoint of beauty and historic interest.) Anyone who works very long in the thick of church life can think up some new criticisms which apparently have not occurred to those who have made church-baiting their avocation. At any rate, he is not disposed to argue the more common complaints against the church, for he recognizes truth in most of them.

Now that a free church no longer exists in some lands that have been the historic ground of Christianity, and the existence of a free church can in no land be taken for granted, the criticisms of the church which have been worn threadbare are overshadowed by the new appreciation of what the church is and what the church means to the world. We remember now that the New Testament originated in the life of the church, and that those who want to separate New Testament Christianity from the church are trying to put asunder what God hath joined together. We remember that the church has been the soil which has nourished Christian character. As Evelyn Underhill has written: "It is often assumed that 'God can bring forth His saints anywhere.' But history and psychology seem to oppose this view. The great saints have mostly arisen within the religious system they were destined to adorn, and their debts to the deepest and most stable elements in that system—especially its tradition of prayer and self-discipline—have been great." [1] We re-

[1] *Hibbert Journal*, April 1932.

member that in full view of all the influences in human life
which tend to break the human family up into hostile,
antagonistic groups, the Christian church has been pro-
jected by an inner dynamic across the world spreading the
faith that one God is the Father of all men, who are therefore in the intention of God if not in practice, brothers. We
remember that wrapped up in this universal gospel is the
faith which has given a new dignity to the individual. Sometimes the preaching of that gospel has produced unexpected
results. Professor Alfred N. Whitehead [2] has expressed the
belief that the final effective force in the abolition of slavery
in Britain was the preaching of the Wesleyans, who were not
primarily concerned with slavery at all, but with preparing
men's souls for a future life. Their preaching, however,
created a new conviction that every man, however debased,
had worth in the sight of God, and under the impact of that
faith the institution of slavery collapsed and disappeared
from the British Isles. We remember that the Christian
church, with all its inconsistencies carrying it again and again
into dogmatic authoritarianism, has been through its gospel
the well-spring out of which human freedom has flowed, so
that, as John Henry Newman said in an earlier day, "Not a
man in Europe who talks bravely against the church but
owes it to the church that he can talk at all." [3] We remember
that through a mechanistic era, when the sheer weight of
machinery has threatened to overwhelm the spiritual life of
man, or at least to delude him into the curious belief that
just because machinery bulks so large in the modern world

[2] *Adventures of Ideas*, pp. 27-8.
[3] *Historical Sketches*, quoted in *Fine Gold of Newman*, edited by
J. J. Reilly, p. 21.

he too must be a machine, the Christian church has gone on preaching, "Now are we the sons of God, and it doth not yet appear what we shall be." [4] We remember that in an age in which man has worshipped himself, or the work of his own hands, or his ancestors, or some so-called super-man, the Christian church has held up before the world a Carpenter from Nazareth, and all unworthily has proclaimed that the God whom Christ reveals is alone deserving of the worship of true men. We remember that in a world over which the night sometimes falls swiftly, where even long life is but a moment between the mysteries of our birth and our death, the church has kept on opening windows through which comes the light of a Sun that never sets, from realms where the day never ends. A jaunty, carefree, cocksure era may neglect these things, but a time like our own regards these faiths with a new appreciation of the fact that through the years God has been speaking through the church the Word that is life.

Mr. George Bernard Shaw wrote some years ago that, "if the people suddenly found themselves without churches and rituals, many of them would find that they had been deprived of a necessity of life; that the want would have to be supplied; and there would presently be more churches than ever and fuller ones. The only people who can do without churches are the simple materialists on the one hand and, on the other, those who have no use for institutional worship because their churches are their own souls." [5] In his earlier years Mr. Shaw wrote that he liked churches best when they

[4] I John 3:2.
[5] *Plain Talk.* Quoted from newspaper review (unidentified).

were empty.[6] This strikes a somewhat different note. The
churches have owed a great debt to Mr. Shaw, because whatever his religious views may have been he has never been
able to keep away from the subject of religion, and he has
kept asking the churches embarrassing questions which have
been good for the church's soul. But is he right when he says
that there are people who can do without churches because
their churches are their own souls? Is not this the reappear-
ance in very faint disguise of a very old friend, the man who
says, "I do not need the church because I can worship best
alone?" Does it not overlook the fact that the man who
feels that religion is an exclusively private affair between himself and God is the very man who most needs fellowship
with other people in worship? It may be true that "religion
is what the individual does with his own solitariness," [7] but
what a man does with his solitariness depends a great deal
upon the fellowships in which his life is set, and what he
does with solitary worship depends a great deal on whether
or not his solitary worship is one aspect of a rich experience
of which another aspect is worship in fellowship with other
people. Are there not ranges in the Christian faith concerning God into which we can enter only in fellowship with
other people who worship Him? Referring to the new
emphasis upon the church as a corporate fellowship which
the Oxford Movement of the nineteenth century brought
about, Evelyn Underhill has observed: "The Evangelical
mind tends to present spiritual experience as a duet. For the
Catholic mind it is, or should be, a symphony; and now
English Christians heard once more the great orchestration

[6] *An Essay on Going to Church* (J. W. Luce & Co., Boston, 1905).
[7] A. N. Whitehead, *Religion in the Making*, p. 16.

of the communion of Saints." [8] We need not bother about
the labels, Evangelical and Catholic. All Christian experience needs for its enrichment that orchestration as an aid
to its understanding of God, and as an affirmation of the
solidarity of mankind before God. In one of Sigrid Undset's
novels, a woman declines her husband's invitation to go to
church with him, saying, "No thanks, let me worship God in
private, if you please." He replies with rare insight, "But
one can do that too, Bjorg. I can worship God as much as
I like when I am alone. But I'm not sure that what I most
need to learn at present isn't this—that God is everyone's
God, and that what I wish God to be for me, God Himself
wishes to be for all, without respect of persons. So I ought
to rejoice in every human being who pays Him adoration,
and I ought to be grateful to anyone who may say to me,
Come, let us worship . . ." [9] There are some words that
even God speaks only to those who approach Him as a
fellowship.

II

This is not to say that the church is not a problem as well
as a necessity. Sometimes at great church gatherings when
he hears the church spoken of in exalted terms as the universal spiritual fellowship of Christ's followers of all generations, a man's mind wanders off to some particular church
that he knows, and he has qualms when he tries to believe
that God has ordained the church to be His messenger to
men. He may believe, with liberal theologians, that Jesus
was the Founder of the Church, not because he actually set

[8] "The Oxford Movement," *Hibbert Journal*, April 1932.
[9] *The Burning Bush*, p. 133.

it up as an organization, but because it arose inevitably out of his message of the Kingdom of God; or he may hold with Continental Europeans that along with the family and the state, the church is one of the orders through which God by fiat has decreed that human life should be governed; or he may accept the view of certain church bodies that Christ commanded the organization of the church in the particular forms which they believe have been followed ever since in their communions. And yet, as he looks at some particular church with its apparent lethargy of spirit, its absorption in the elementary business of making ends meet, its zeal for new members not as souls to be saved, but as potential contributors to the budget, its slavery to old ways and reluctance to receive new ideas or to follow new paths, its placidity as the custodian of a gospel meant to turn the world upside down—he wonders. Of course that is not a true picture of any church, however complacent it may look on the surface. "How do you stand being the minister of these smug people?" a young collegian asked a ministerial acquaintance. The minister thought of those people, not as the collegian saw them when he was home for the holidays, ranged in rows in the pews of the church on a Sunday morning. He thought of them as he knew them at close range, human beings with their share of faults, but men and women who had seen a light that they followed, who were, many of them, carrying sorrows with a quiet heroism, who were in unostentatious ways doing constructive things to make their community a better place, who were giving money with a generosity which in proportion to their means was astonishing, who were the first people to be called on when some need arose and who were the last people to demand public recognition for the community service which they rendered, who went home from church on Sundays to homes where there was a quality of idealism quite distinct from the shoddy advertising of many other families, and who went on Monday mornings to places of business and professional life which they knew were far from the kingdom of God but where they were making an honest attempt to introduce and work out the spirit of Christ. The minister said to himself that these so-called smug people were better Christians than he was, and that he was proud to be their minister. He remembered that he had read that a church "is not a society of select persons, but the home and school both of saints and sinners," [10] and he was glad that the church he served was of that kind. And yet he, like all thoughtful churchmen, knew that the church is a problem as well as a necessity.

No one who loves the church can fail to be disturbed by the fact that it does not exert a more powerful influence than it does upon the social order. No one who cares deeply about the church can view without regret the cleavages that run through individual churches, to say nothing of the church at large. (Bishop Gore used to say that the word "ecclesiastical" ought to mean "brotherly." [11]) No loyal churchman can be anything but sorrowful as he lets his mind dwell on the tasks confronting the Christian church today, and then thinks of the actual churches that he knows, many of them struggling, impoverished, far from impressive as the world ordinarily measures the power of institutions. How shall he adjust himself to this situation in which he finds himself both critic and lover of the church, proud and

[10] F. R. Barry, *The Relevance of the Church*, p. 67.
[11] *Ibid.*, p. 222.

ashamed, confident supporter and yet aware of its failures
and weaknesses? He can at least remember that the church is
something more than the sum total of the existing churches,
with their strengths and their weaknesses. The conferences
are right when they say that the church is the spiritual
fellowship of Christ's people transcending the lines which
time and geography and organization and tradition have
created. The church is the body of Christ, and God has
spoken and does speak to mankind through His Church.
It was the weekly magazine, *Time*, in its Christmas issue
of a few years ago, which made one of the most discerning
of contemporary comments on the significance of the
Christian church. After reviewing the activities of Christian
churches in a year of foreboding and gathering storm, the
magazine said:

"In a world much burdened with unreligious and anti-
religious deeds, the Church,—the myriad churches and sects
which believe they follow Christ—had become immeasurably
greater for what it was than for what it might attempt to do.
In spite of its apparent disunity, the Church alone among
human institutions, stood for the universal brotherhood of
man, the unity of the human race. To that far ideal the
Church still kept its faith; on Christmas 1938 took courage
once again from the oldest and dearest story it knew." [12]

III

Such a comment reminds us, as busy churchmen need
continually to be reminded, that the church is a historic
fellowship. Mrs. Miniver, that sprightly philosopher of the
common life, has observed that in motoring one's success

[12] *Time*, December 26, 1938.

as a driver involves keeping an eye on a mirrored image of the road behind while one speeds ahead, a practice which she says is advisable in other aspects of life besides motoring.[13] There have been times when the church was accused, perhaps justly, of looking too much into the mirror and too little at the road ahead. Most churches probably err today on the side of paying too little attention to the Christian tradition out of which they have come. The church must of course address itself to the contemporary needs of our own time. When any church tries to live in the past it is a sure sign that the reports of its approaching demise cannot be exaggerated. But a church which is merely contemporary, with no stabilizing and stimulating awareness of its own tradition, is a church which has lost perspective. The symbols and the sacraments of the church link us with a long past, a past full of trouble and tragedy, of sin and sorrow, of struggle and shame, through all of which there has existed as a productive center of life this fellowship of people who have confronted it all with a glowing faith that what God can do in human life and wills to do for human life has been interpreted to us in Christ. Contemporary life bristles with questions, at the heart of which is the central question which the old hymn answers with a glance at Christian history:

> "Finding, following, keeping, struggling,
> Is He sure to bless?
> Saints, apostles, prophets, martyrs
> Answer yes!"

Like mountain-climbers who are often buried in clouds which come down and settle around them hiding the peaks,

[13] Jan Struther, *Mrs. Miniver*, p. 120.

but who can still see beneath their feet the trail beaten on the mountain-side by the feet of those who through the generations have climbed the mountain before them, so again and again in the confusion of contemporary life, the wayfaring Christian finds guidance and hope in the knowledge that he makes the steep ascent as part of a historic fellowship.

IV

One of the hopeful factors in the contemporary situation is the growing awareness of the church as an ecumenical fellowship. If we are sometimes discouraged that progress toward a united church is so slow, it may comfort us to remember that there has been progress. When Dr. Johnson and his Boswell were about to set out on their tour to the Hebrides, they stopped in Calder at the manse of the Presbyterian minister, a Mr. McAulay (whose library, incidentally, Dr. Johnson inspected, but "thought it rather a lady's library, with some Latin books in it by chance, than the library of a clergyman."). Household prayers presented a problem, as Boswell did not think that the Doctor would be present at a Presbyterian prayer. There was a discussion as to whether Dr. Johnson should be asked to sit in the library while the Presbyterians prayed elsewhere, or whether prayers should be omitted altogether, as Mr. McAulay considerately suggested. The matter was finally presented to the Doctor, who consented to hear the prayer. "This was a pleasing surprise to me;" wrote Boswell, "for he refused to go and hear Principal Robertson preach. 'I will hear him [said he] if he will get up into a tree to preach; but I will not give a sanction, by my presence, to a Presbyterian assembly.' " [14] However we may lament the passing of some aspects of the Age of Johnson, we can be thankful that Anglicans and Presbyterians, and all other families of Christians, can worship together, on certain occasions at least, in our time.

It is of course possible to exaggerate the significance of the world-wide interconnections which have been painfully and slowly established among the churches. The fact that the churches in both Germany and the United States have contacts with Geneva should not be permitted to blind us to the horror of the fact that Christians in Germany and Christians in America are at war with each other, and under certain circumstances are in duty bound to slay each other. The American Christian believes that through the war he is seeking the welfare of his Christian brothers in Germany as well as in his own country, and he is thankful that when this war engulfed our nations there was for Protestants a center of cooperative activity in Switzerland, as there was for Catholic churches in Rome, with which communication could be maintained. But that accentuates rather than minimizes the terrible nature of the disruption which the war represents. In a volume published in preparation for the Oxford Conference in 1937, it was suggested that, "if it be true that it is possible for a man to be a communist and a Christian, or a fascist and a Christian, then it would seem to be possible—to take the most extreme instance—that those who hold these conflicting allegiances should meet in the morning at the

[14] James Boswell, *The Journal of a Tour to the Hebrides with Samuel Johnson,* pp. 102-3 (J. M. Dent).

altar and later in the day at the barricades." [15] It would be
hard to imagine a more gruesome picture of the church's
predicament in modern society. We have not yet resolved
the difficulty which confronts men with a common religious
allegiance when their divergent political loyalties have involved them in violence. The fact that they do have a common altar should not be used as an opiate to dull their sense
of pain over the contradiction between the altar and the bar-
ricade. The existence of ecumenical contacts has certain very
practical advantages during this period of war. It gives us a
chance to maintain a measure of understanding among Christians of warring nations. It gives us new opportunities to express the Christian spirit of mercy through the churches on
an international scale. It gives us the assurance that the structure of a world-wide church has already been begun, and that
when the war is over it must be carried forward to completion. Sometimes, however, one is disturbed by hearing references to the ecumenical church which seem to imply that
the growing fellowship of the churches somehow mitigates
the tragedy of a world conflict in which Christian people are
involved. On the contrary it deepens the tragedy and brings
out into bolder relief the horror of it.

Nevertheless, for the future this ecumenical spirit which
has been growing in the churches is one of the signs of hope.
If Christianity is to help to unify a broken and disordered
world, it must show sufficient wisdom and grace to unify a
divided and disordered Christendom. The provisional organization of the World Council of Churches, the continuing
service of the Central Bureau for the Relief of European

[15] W. A. Visser 't Hooft and J. H. Oldham, *The Church and Its
Function in Society*, p. 215.

Churches, the unique spirit which exists in the World Student Christian Federation, these signs of a new discovery of the larger meanings of the Christian faith, transcending the lines of sect and nation and race, are promises of a day when religion, which because of its intensity can be one of the most divisive of influences, will serve as a bond of the spirit enabling a world that is weary of its wars and commotions to live together in peace.

There are two avenues along which the movements toward a united church can move. One of them is unofficial, the other official. One of them is through an informal development of interest among individuals, the other is through formal organization. Neither is complete without the other. When the Conference on Life and Work met at Oxford in 1937, it was commonly said that one of its greatest contributions was the happy discovery of the depth of the Christian unity which already existed among those who gathered in that city of domes and spires, a unity which was manifest especially in the daily worship at St. Mary's Church. That was a unity which required the vote of no ecclesiastical bodies. It was there, in the spirits of men. There is far more of that kind of Christian unity in the world today than we officially recognize. Shall we say that there is more of it among laymen than among ministers, or that there is more of it among laymen who do not hold official positions in churches than among those who have been long in the harness as office-bearers? That would not be true, perhaps. But it is true that the doctrinal and organizational matters around which official discussions of Christian unity revolve in circumlocutions which seem to approach perpetual motion, have scant interest for many laymen who are most deeply concerned with the Christian church and the Christian cause. Sometimes the layman is not disposed to wait until great ecclesiastical bodies, which like other great bodies move slowly, have resolved their differences with regard to creeds and rituals and orders. He hopes that they will get together, but he is not sure that he will live to see that happy day. In the meantime he has his life to live, and he wants to live it in the Christian church. He has a short-cut to Christian unity. He can identify himself with the local church which he finds most congenial, the church in which he can render the best service, regardless of its denominational affiliation, and in doing so he can feel that he is in touch with the universal Christian fellowship which is the church. That is what he is doing in great numbers. The number of people in the average local church who have had experience as members of churches in other communions is very large, and is constantly increasing. In any community where there is considerable coming and going, it is almost the usual thing for newcomers, if they identify themselves with churches at all, to do so on the basis of what seems to meet their present need rather than on the basis of their previous denominational membership. Sometimes of course this merely indicates that the church does not mean very much to them, and therefore it makes little difference to which church they belong. In every movement toward Christian unity the question must always be asked, "Have the old differences lost their intensity because the churches themselves have lost their intensity, or have the old differences been transcended by a larger loyalty and a larger vision of Christian truth?" Sometimes the layman has lost interest in his denomination because he has lost interest in the church. But very often these people move across denominational lines because their real interest is in something in which every Christian church is interested. They care very much about the church, and their loyalty is one of the greatest assets which the church of Christ has in the world today.

It is this body of informal interest in Christian unity which is sometimes forgotten in the official approaches to the task of uniting the churches. It is this group of people that the official method of seeking unity sometimes alienates. For it is one of the strange paradoxes of our present situation that the ecumenical movement has in some ways revivified the spirit of denominationalism while it has been trying to find ways of uniting the denominations into one organic church. When people of this type are asked to meet with people of other denominations, each to describe to the other the peculiar virtues of his own religious group, these people may decline on the ground that they are not interested in that—they are interested in what the Christian church can do to meet the world's need—or, if they do enter into such discussion, they may develop a spirit of denominational pride which they did not have before. When inter-denominational bodies are set up, as they must be set up, through representation of the official bodies of the denominations, these people are not in any real sense represented. No official ecclesiastical body in the United States today really represents the mind of its constituency, whether it be a Presbytery, a Conference, a Diocese, a Classis or some other official group. The attempt to have the ecumenical movement rooted in the churches by building it upon the legally constituted ecclesiastical structures, inevitable as that method is, is deceptive, since so large a share of the most enlightened and most devoted laity are completely out of touch with any church machinery beyond that of the local church, and would be startled, puzzled, or amused to be informed that a convention or conference was entitled to speak for them. If we are to have orderly church processes, it must be through legally constituted bodies that the church speaks, and the ecumenical movement must be founded upon them, rather than be found floating off into the void with no visible means of support, financial, spiritual or organizational. But the elected or appointed delegates of the churches always do well to remember this large, more or less inarticulate, but deeply interested section of their constituencies. Like the delegates at Oxford, we need to remember that we already have a much larger measure of Christian unity than is officially recognized. When the official movements for the unity of the Christian church seem to be unable to advance beyond some point of doctrine or procedure, we need to remember this large group of unofficial Christians who are mainly concerned with translating the Christian faith into Christian life in a terribly unchristian world. Perhaps we can even dare believe that God has a word to speak to His world through them.

V

We have this ecumenical spirit in the church today because the church has always been a missionary movement. It could not have been otherwise with a church preaching the Christian gospel. The missionary movement is not, as is sometimes supposed, a program which has been added on to the Christian church. It is inherent in the very nature of the church's faith. Given a faith in a God who is universal, and an ethic centering in the obligation of altruism, and you have the ingredients of a missionary movement. When that faith becomes a personal loyalty to a Master whose supreme concern was that all men should know God as their Father, and when for the obligation of altruism is substituted the dynamic of the Cross on which that Master died with a love on his lips and in his heart that has universal significance, then a missionary movement ceases to be merely an obligation and becomes an irresistible enthusiasm. It was as inevitable that the Christian church should have become an expanding movement as that light should radiate or that the wind should blow. That is not to say that the human agents employed in the expansion of Christianity have always been wise in their methods or enlightened in their doctrine. Fortunately the gospel is God's treasure even when in earthen vessels, and its radiance shines through the imperfections of its interpreters, if they embody its essential spirit. I owe a deep debt to Dr. Doremus Scudder who impressed that fact upon my mind one memorable evening in Tokyo years ago, when I had been bumptiously voicing my callow criticisms of the theology of a group of missionaries whom I had met on a steamer, and he quietly told me just what those people were doing in the way of Christlike service to human need in the slums of his city, and how their life interpreted the heart of their gospel more eloquently than any theology could hope to do. Let the church re-examine its methods and the forms in which its message is stated. Let the re-examination be made without fear and without evasion ·generation after generation. Two thousand years of missionary history look down upon the present and assure us that wherever men have been really captured by Christian truth, God will be speaking in varied ways through them to other people.

The need for a church as a world-wide fellowship is apparent to a larger company than ever in these times. A native pastor in the Cameroun last December was trying to express to a visiting American what the church means in the world. His language was inadequate, and he fell back on sign-talk, linking the forefingers of his two hands together as symbols of his belief that the churches of the world are links in a great chain of faith "holding the world together." [16] Anyone who thinks that faith is important can see the importance of that.

So obvious is this strand in Christian history, that it may seem unnecessary to lay this emphasis upon it. But it is not obvious to a large segment of the contemporary church. Many local churches and some communions are so organized as to make it appear that the maintenance of local work is a requirement but the wider ministry of the church is optional. It is assumed by many people that the carrying on of the church's work in the immediate community is a task in which everyone should share, but that the extension of the church's service is for the few who for some inscrutable reason have that particular interest. There is a widespread prejudice, even within the church family, against the word *missionary*. Attempts are being made to substitute other words for it, and to talk about "world service," "world fellowship," and "world community." Insofar as these new terms help to explain the universalism of the Christian church to people who have been blinded by misconceptions of the missionary movement, they have value. There is something rather puzzling, however, about this newly discovered enthusiasm for the world Christian community on the part of some people who would be very much embarrassed to be found marching

[16] Letter of Dr. Charles T. Leber and Dr. Phillips P. Elliott; January 11, 1942.

under the banner of missions, inasmuch as there would be no world Christian community today except for the existence of the so-called "younger churches" which are the fruitage of the missionary movement, and especially of the missionary expansion of the nineteenth century, as has been so convincingly demonstrated by Professor Kenneth S. Latourette.[17] A world community does not just happen. It does not take root and grow of itself. It is the product of missions, and a missionary is "one sent." Behind the missionary movement is the creative and redemptive will of God, and no new vocabulary should be permitted to obscure the basic fact of which the missionary movement is the expression, that through the expansion of the Christian church God is speaking to His world.

VI

Sometimes, however, a minister has a suspicion that the problem of creating a real fellowship in one congregation is almost as difficult as that of creating a world Christian community. Quantitatively it is a smaller task, but qualitatively it is the same problem. Certainly we can have no world Christian community which does not rest upon the foundation of strong local churches which have achieved a spirit of Christian community in their own life. It may be that at the present time the Christian movement as a whole is top-heavy, stronger in the great movements which command the headlines than in the ordinary churches which have to hold the line but which are too often very weak in the light of the challenge which confronts them. At any rate, it can be said

[17] *History of the Expansion of Christianity:* Vol. IV, *The Great Century.*

without reservation that the strength of the Christian church as a fellowship is the strength of the local churches that compose it.

The existence of small local fellowships of people who have learned to live, think, work and worship together as communities has an importance far out of proportion to the size of these groups. In the *Christian News-Letter*, published at Oxford in 1941, Mr. G. D. H. Cole discussed what he called the problem of "Democracy Face to Face with Hugeness." During the greater part of the history of civilized living, he pointed out, men have been used to living together in quite small groups. Only quite recently have men been faced with decisions involving the actions of millions of people, and been confronted by problems which in their magnitude and complexity have outrun man's present capacity for collective control. It has been during this period of an expanding community of interest that democracy has grown up. What chance is there that democratic procedures can cope with such a situation? "Our problem," says Mr. Cole, "is simple to state. It is to find democratic ways of living for little men in big societies. . . . Democracy can work in the great State (and a *fortiori* between great States or over Europe or the world) only if each State is made up of a host of little democracies, and rests finally, not on isolated individuals, but on groups small enough to express the spirit of neighborhood and personal acquaintance." [18] Wholly aside from their other functions, local churches are in a unique position to be such seed-plots in which the tender plants of democratic life can take root and thrive.

In order to be such a fellowship, however, a church must

[18] Issue of July 16, 1941.

fuse together in one spirit a variety of people whom the ordinary tendencies of secular life would divide into separate compartments. Of course, a church can evade this problem by building its membership from people who come from only one of these secular compartments. Too many churches are made up of people whose economic status, social outlook, tastes and habits are pretty much the same. On the part of many churches, this social uniformity has been an unconscious development, due to the fact that the churches stand in neighborhoods which have been subjected to the same pressure for uniformity. The influence of real estate values upon theology would be an interesting subject for study. This is not the occasion for that, but it can be observed that zoning ordinances, tax rates, and property valuations do draw people of similar circumstances into the same geographical neighborhoods, and that the mind of particular churches is profoundly influenced by such groupings. One of the services which the automobile has rendered the church is that it has lessened the importance of geographical proximity to the particular church with which a person maintains his affiliation, and thereby makes possible a cross-fertilization of churches with the outlook of different geographical communities. This complicates the problems of church administration, but it enriches the life and work of the churches fortunate enough to draw upon such variety in their memberships. For it is an incalculable loss when any church becomes a class church. After listening to Catharine Breshkovskaya speaking at Wellesley College in 1904, Miss Vida Scudder wrote: "Listening to episode after episode, conviction grew that the worst prison in the world is privileged class consciousness; and that if one could escape, as she had done, suffocating within those invisible walls, physical imprisonment such as she had suffered might be a charter of liberty." [19] That such class consciousness has been found within the fellowship of the church is no secret. When Charles Simeon's evangelical preaching drew crowds of underprivileged people to Trinity Church, Cambridge, in 1782, the pewholders locked up their pews and stayed at home. He preached to them, nevertheless, as they stood in the aisles. He put benches in the aisles for them to sit on, which the church wardens promptly threw into the churchyard.[20] One can hardly imagine such an incident today, but in these days of passive resistance (which can be used to resist good as well as evil purposes) there are subtler ways of achieving the same result. Merely bringing people into the same building or putting their names on the same membership roll does not of itself create a fellowship. It may only intensify friction. Ivan, in *The Brothers Karamazov*, says: "I could never understand how one can love his neighbors. It's just neighbors, to my mind, that one can't love, though one might love those at a distance." [21] People from different backgrounds can be brought together into a fellowship only when their common loyalty and their common faith unite them in a purpose which is stronger than the divisive forces that pull them apart. A local church therefore can become a center of democratic life to the extent that it is permeated by the conviction that God speaks not only to the church but through the church as a spiritual fellowship.

It should be recognized that it is just the conviction that God speaks through His church which has sometimes mili-

[19] *On Journey*, p. 158.
[20] Constance Padwyck, *Life of Henry Martyn*, p. 65.
[21] Feodor Dostoievski, *The Brothers Karamazov*, Book V, Chap. 4.

tated against the spirit of fellowship in the church. It is possible even for saints to differ as to just what God is saying at a
particular time through the church. The authoritarian
churches have attempted to avoid this difficulty through
formal creeds, but someone must always interpret the creed,
and the application of its principles to new situations and
new knowledge is not always simple. Free churches have
sometimes tried to avoid this difficulty by becoming so free as
to be nebulous in their beliefs. If that solves one problem, it
creates others, for experience has shown that nebulous convictions are ineffective convictions. As H. G. Wells wrote, "A
community where binding beliefs have decayed altogether is
like a building whose mortar has been changed to sand. It
may stand fast for a time, but it stands precariously." [22] To
maintain freedom, firm convictions, and fellowship in one
church is a task which requires intelligence, a sense of humor,
common sense, and Christian grace. Alexander Whyte stated
the formula for this delicate task as clearly as it can be put
when he said, apropos of church controversy: "For the re-
straint of controversy, for the reign of peace, and for the life
of love, I would willingly become almost all things to all men.
But you will say to me in triumph that truth is truth. And so
it is. But I say also—that love is love. And I have the highest
authority for it, that love is the fulfilling of every law: the law
of truth, and the law of duty, and every other law." [23]

The answer to many of the problems involved in the creation of fellowship in a local church lies in making it a working community. People of a wide variety of social, political,
and intellectual viewpoints can be drawn together into real

[22] *The Open Conspiracy*, p. 4.
[23] G. F. Barbour, *Alexander Whyte*, p. 438.

unity when they are engaged together in common tasks big enough to command the allegiance of all. People of different theological backgrounds can find that they have deep things in common when they are working together for ends in which they all believe. Of course it is not true that the busiest church is necessarily the most useful church. Even church people can be busy about things that are not very important. A church, like any other organization, can mistake activity for accomplishment, and can forget that the places where light and power are generated are not the noisiest places to be found. The great business of the church will always be transacted in the silent places out of sight of human eye, and the ordinary methods of statistics, cataloguing, and advertising can never describe it. The distinctive thing about the church must always be that it is a worshipping community, but just as it is true that "he prayeth best who loveth best," so it is also true that a church will have a deeper reality in its worship if it is also a working community.

A local church may well set for its goal the ideal of having every member enlisted in some form of church work. But that ideal needs to be interpreted with discretion. It is a waste of good material for a church to manufacture little jobs and then dragoon into them men who would prefer to be doing something that seems to them more vital. The "make-work fallacy" is as deceptive in ecclesiastical affairs as it is in economics. It is misleading and self-defeating when in the face of the world's colossal needs, the church absorbs people's time in little jobs. That is not to say that ushering on Sunday morning cannot be done with such a fine sense of the privilege of worship that it becomes a high ministry, or that so much Christian friendship cannot be expressed with needle and thread that sewing becomes a work of grace! But no one should be employed by the church in a task which he does not see as a Christian ministry. The familiar practice of thinking up jobs and then putting pressure on busy people to take jobs that would not exist except for someone's zeal to "put everybody at work" is one of the blunders which has put a barrier between the church and many of the ablest people, whose services the church needs. One of the most useful women in her city once complained that she had done all her work outside the church because her church had offered her only little tasks while other agencies in the city were demanding the very great executive abilities which she was generally recognized to possess.

Let it be said with great emphasis that there is need for a revaluation upward of some of the tasks in the church which are often undervalued. When a man refuses to invest time and thought and life with a group of boys when he obviously has the gifts for such leadership (rare gifts they are!) because something else seems to him more important, one wants to ask, "What is there outside your own family that could possibly be more important?" Christian faith must leap from life to life, and the existence of groups where such transfer can take place is of paramount importance, if the Christian faith is important. There are a good many functions in the church on which the life of the church depends, and no one with an appreciation of the church's significance can regard them as of slight moment.

Even so, we may well give some thought to a re-interpretation of what we mean by "church work." Every community is served by social and cultural agencies which contribute services which once were functions of the church—hospitals,

schools, welfare societies, Christian Associations and the like.
They were born in the church, they express a spirit which is
the fruitage of the church, and they do the kind of thing that
Christ would be doing if he were in our midst in visible form.
They are independent of ecclesiastical control for the most
part, and it is good that they are. The church as an institution
has all the administrative work that it can carry without attempting to administer the healing, educational and social
work of the community. These agencies and institutions
could not exist without the leadership, cooperation and support of the people who are in the churches, to say nothing of
the impetus of the religious faith of a former generation
which still impels their secular descendants into social welfare enterprises, although they have sometimes parted company with the religious faith in which these enterprises originated. (The children of the secular generation, be it said in
passing, are in considerable numbers turning back to the religious faith of their grandparents and great-grandparents,
with some feeling that they have been badly served by those
who exposed them to a wildly turbulent era with no adequate
faith with which to confront it.) Nothing could be more unfortunate than to have the feeling prevail, as it does prevail
in some quarters, that social work and the church are compet-
ing for the time and interest of an individual Christian. Social
work is church work, whether or not the social worker or the
churchman is willing to have it so labeled. It is the kind of
work which the church has always existed to do in the spirit of
a Lord who was a Healer, a Teacher, a Personal Counsellor, a
Friend in the richest human sense, as well as Saviour, Re-
deemer, Prophet, Priest, and King. The local church should
recognize that its people are doing church work through such

social agencies, as well as when they are within the four walls of the church building doing things that are under the supervision of ecclesiastically selected church officers. Every church may well tabulate such services rendered by its people, include them in its annual reports as part of the work which the church is doing, and officially recognize the fact that a large part of the work which the church does is in a sense unofficial. Such recognition will deepen the conviction among its members that the church is a working fellowship.

There will always be abundant opportunities for the church to be doing things that no one else will do or can do. There will be some tasks in which the church can pioneer and awaken the public conscience to needs of which it was not keenly aware, as it has done in the case of the lepers, of migrants, and others. There will be some tasks where the church must hang on and keep some services going after the tasks have lost the romance of novelty and other people have let go, as the churches did with Near East Relief after the last war. There will always be need for the people of the churches to be thinking their way out into new problems and to be facing them with the mind of Christ, as many church people are trying to do today with the intricate problems of labor, of race cooperation, of international justice, and all the medley of problems that will confront the world at the ending of the war. Much of this kind of church work can be done best in groups that are not too large. It is a fairly good rough and ready rule for a church to resolve never to have in its organization a group that it can get along without. If it is alive and alert to its opportunities, it will be surprising how many groups form around some common interest or some common task. If care is taken that they be organized around interests

and tasks, they need never become mere cliques within the
church, creating social divisiveness and disunity. A working
church may have wide diversity in its activities, and still have
all its manifold life center in its main purpose. As Dr. William S. Rainsford wrote of the Church House at St. George's
Church in New York City: "It should be a teaching house
and a dancing house; a reading house and a playing house;
and because it was these, it should be a preaching house, bidding the neighborhood look for, strive for, and believe in a
better manhood and a better day." [24]

VII

All of which is to say that the church is by its very nature a
fellowship in Christ. That is what finally distinguishes it
from all other associations of human beings. Whether we
think of the churches as gathered out of society for purposes
of worship and mutual service, or as coming down through
the centuries one corporate body through the laying on of
hands by properly accredited leaders of the church, Christ is
the common center. He gathers the churches around himself,
and he is the continuing spirit making the churches of succeeding generations one church. If he is the revelation of
God's purpose, then the church has its origin in the purpose
of God, for the church was the inevitable outcome of his
mission. As Bishop Barry has said: "Here the eternal purpose
of redemption clothes itself in visible form on earth. In a
world of alienation and antagonism where men felt that they
were estranged from God, a new society woke into life by the
touch of God through Christ in the Gospel. In it the barriers
were down, and in mutual trust and forgiveness men learnt

[24] *The Story of a Varied Life: An Autobiography*, p. 215.

the meaning of the divine love. It was something unprecedented and unique; no fortunate accident of history, but the work of God whose will for the world—to call men into fellowship with Himself through Christ and thereby with one another—was thus being revealed and fulfilled. It was the divine will coming true on earth as it is in heaven. This is the heart of Christian experience; it is what Christ means in the lives of men." [25] That is a theological statement of our faith that the church is the body of our fellowship in Christ. A more human statement of the same truth is found in a fragment of a letter Maxwell Chaplin wrote from Hwai Yuen years ago, when theological controversy in this country was rife: "How far away and how futile all theological discussions seemed the other day as I sat with that little company of Christians in the chill, dirty little village schoolroom, with its dirt floor and paper windows, and listened to the pastor as he broke the bread and poured out the wine for the communion service." [26]

In the "blitz" the Scottish church of St. Columba, on Pont Street in London, was destroyed by bombs. On the Sunday morning following its destruction, a member of the congregation went to the spot where the church had stood, where only a bit of broken wall remained. On that wall, the minister had posted a notice stating where the usual morning service would be held that day. Beneath that notice someone had written the verse which appears in Latin around the burning bush on the seal of the Church of Scotland, "Nec tamen consumebatur." The man who wrote that notice believed that the church is more than stone and bricks and mortar. It is

[25] The Relevance of the Church, p. 56
[26] Letters of Maxwell Chaplin, edited by George Stewart, p. 183.

more than organization and ritual and schedules of services. It is the faith and life of men and women to whom the Word of God has come with power, and through whom that Word is mediated to the world.[27] "Heaven and earth shall pass away, but my words shall not pass away." [28]

[27] *Life and Work,* Magazine of the Church of Scotland.
[28] Matthew 24:35.

III

THE WORD AND THE WORLD

"The seed is the word of God."

LUKE 8:11.

"The field is the world."

MATTHEW 13:38.

THE WORD AND THE WORLD

CHRISTIANITY in our time has confidently believed that the Word of God, when heard and obeyed, has power to transform the world and to make human life a fellowship of the children of God. There have been eras when that faith was not conspicuous, even in the Christian church. At times the Word of God has been interpreted almost exclusively as the hope of salvation for the individual in another world beyond this. Sometimes Christians have felt that the Word of God was a command to leave the world of the common life, and to set up select communities apart from the common life where by excluding sinful men (not always a successful endeavor) a group life could be ordered by Christian teachings. But in our time a mighty hope for a transformed world has surged through the Christian community, and men have believed that the Word of God is a command to seek the kingdom of God in the common life of today. The preacher can afford to leave to the scholars the endless debates as to what Jesus meant by the kingdom of God. He will probably assume that Jesus meant what he seems to mean in the gospel records, a new order of life in which the will of God will be done on earth as it is in heaven. The preacher understands that the whole matter bristles with unanswered questions. What is the will of God? Can there ever be a perfect life on the earth where everything grows and is therefore incomplete? If it is the good pleasure of God to give His

children the Kingdom, what can men do about it? These and
countless other questions rise and will keep rising in every
inquiring mind. Nevertheless the preacher of the Word of
God finds that the heart of the message which he feels called
to preach is not dependent upon the finality of his answers to
these questions. He does not expect to know all about the
will of God on this earth, but he does believe that Christ is
the window through which light comes from God. Whether
there ever can be a perfect life on earth seems like a very aca-
demic question when there are so many obvious places where
life can be made much less imperfect than it now is. God is
the Giver of every good and perfect gift, but so long as many
of God's best gifts are clearly contingent upon the intelligent
and dedicated efforts of men, the preacher will take it for
granted that when Jesus said, "Seek ye the Kingdom," he
meant that in the Providence of God the hard work of men
and women would count for something in the establishment
of the Kingdom. If it is contended that we do not know
enough about the actual words of Jesus to draw deductions
from them, but have in the gospels documents representing
the beliefs of the early church, the preacher who finds such
matters too high for him would still maintain that the New
Testament reveals a personality the whole impress of whose
life has from the beginning prompted men to attempt the
establishment of brotherhood on the earth. No doubt there
have been a good many naive hopes cherished in the name of
the Kingdom of God. Without question, many Protestant
Christians celebrated their deliverance from a belief in original sin with an unwarranted confidence in their own goodness which has led to a deluge of sin that is not very original.
But the very collapse of a civilization which has proved far less

stable than it seemed has made all the more apparent our
need for the Word of God concerning our world.

In the midst of all the controversies over the church's duty
in confronting the social problems which beset the age, one
fact stands clear. Whatever may be the attitudes taken by
the church itself, there is an instinctive feeling on the part of
people in general that the Christian church does have a responsibility for society as well as for individuals. When society breaks down, there is an intuitive conviction that if the
church had done its work better, things could have been
held together. When some conspicuous evil raises its head in
the world, on all sides, and especially among idealistic youth,
the question is raised, "Why doesn't the church take a stand
against that?" (Why it is generally expected that the church
should take a stand against rather than for something is one
of the mysteries.) When the church does not take a stand
sufficiently united and effective to prevent some evil or to
create some desired good, the public verdict is that the
church has failed.

The first duty of the minister is to persuade the church to
plead guilty to that indictment. Let the church confess without evasion that the existence of economic injustice, racial
prejudice, political corruption, and widespread degradation
are evidences that the grace of God has not yet had a chance
through the Christian church to do its perfect work. It might
perhaps be said that one of the purposes for which the church
exists is to be a failure. The church must always be creating in
human life a desire for a better social order than has yet been
achieved. Insofar as that desire is created, the world will turn
back on the church and quite justly hold it responsible for
the gap between the ideals it professes and the meager

achievement to which, when it is honest, it confesses. The
fact that the world expects achievements as well as ideals
from the church is one of the elements in the church's hope.
If men felt that the kind of world in which we live today were
the best that the Christian life of the churches could have
created, we would have to write the church off as a dead issue
in contemporary life. The fact that men instinctively feel
that the church ought to have done better than this is an indication that the church is alive as a force for social righteousness. Professor C. E. M. Joad wrote in a discussion of the failures of Christianity: "The world has a long way to go before
its practices square with its professions, but the first step is for
its professions to condemn its practices, and that step has
been taken." [1] The church must confess that it has failed,
must go on giving its best in an effort to achieve a better
world, knowing that when it has done its best, it will still be
a failure from the standpoint of the Word of God.

II

But the minister must also help the people of his own
church at least to see why the church cannot out of hand
organize the perfect social order into existence, or even speak
to the world with one clear united voice on many contro-
versial social issues. One reason is that the church does not
stand over against the world as a clearly distinguishable en-
tity. The church is made up of people who in addition to being churchmen are also businessmen, lawyers, teachers, government officials, and heads of families. In a sense the church
is a segment of the world, rather than a distinctly separable
group of people. There is a good deal of unreality about some

[1] *The New Statesman,* May 3, 1941.

discussions of what the church ought to say to business or to the state, as though two remote and unacquainted persons were dealing with each other. More often such discussions actually take place within the conscience of one man, as he asks himself what his loyalty to the Christian ideal as a churchman requires of him when he confronts the problems with which he must deal as a businessman or in his profession or as a citizen. If he is a loyal churchman, he must put his loyalty to God before all other loyalties. But these interwoven relationships complicate the task of the church which strives to know and speak the Word of God to the world.

The Protestant church is also confronted by the difficulty of identifying its own voice. Who speaks for the church on social questions? The minister? But there are many ministers, and the last thing that would be said of them is that they are unanimous. The resolutions passed by church assemblies? They are straws showing which way the wind is blowing, but how many laymen in the churches even know that they are passed? Campaigns to get church members to write letters to legislators? The evidence is that such campaigns have been undeniably effective, and yet they constitute a serious problem for our representative form of government, and may in the end be effective in undermining that form of government, putting the actual power in the hands not of the people but of those who control the radio, the mails, and the machinery of large scale propaganda. Plebiscites? Perhaps the time may come when an accurate polling of opinion in Protestant churches may reveal the considered judgment of their membership, but how difficult it is even to state most social issues in a form on which a "Yes" or "No"

answer can honestly be given, and how difficult to get such
votes taken in a church of a million members! Sample ballots, following the modern techniques for interpreting public
opinion? Such ballots would be interesting if we had more
of them, but would even Dr. Gallup claim that such a sam-
pling process can be an authoritative proclamation of the
truth God seeks to express through the churches? The democratic and representative character of the Protestant churches,
which is their strength and their pride, sometimes makes it
difficult to say with assurance who speaks for the churches.

But an even greater difficulty is inherent in the very nature
of Protestantism. The Protestant church is trying, and must
go on trying, to be two things that are mutually contradictory.
It is trying to be a witnessing fellowship, and it is trying to
be a free fellowship. If the church were concerned only with
its witness, it would be an exclusive body, keeping its membership undiluted by those not in hearty agreement with the
positions, theological and social, on which it desires to bear
its testimony. If the church were concerned only with its
freedom, it would be an inclusive society, bidding welcome to
all sincere seekers after truth, and saying to them, "Come,
let us reason together, and together press forward to a larger
knowledge of the Word of God for our generation." But it
must be concerned with both its witness and its freedom at
the same time. This conflict of tendencies in the very nature
of the Protestant church is not generally recognized. The
zealous prophet calls upon the church to keep its freedom
untainted, setting up no tests for membership, either as to
belief or social attitude, and at the same time insists that the
church ought to bear a united and unanimous witness on

some disputed social question, generally assuming that the
church ought to be unanimous in the views on which he, one
man, is unanimous. But free fellowships must necessarily
sacrifice unanimity. Every church has had to strike a compromise between complete freedom and complete agreement. Some, like the Presbyterian church, have restricted
their ministry to those who can agree to certain doctrinal
statements, while leaving wide latitude on social issues.
Some, like the Society of Friends, permit the widest range
of theological belief to office-bearers, but by tradition at least
regard non-participation in war as a tenet of the group. Every
church makes its compromise somewhere between freedom
and agreement, or it would become an amorphous mass of
people standing for nothing and going nowhere. This needs
to be frankly recognized. It also needs to be recognized that
this constitutes a problem for every church which is concerned with being an instrument through which God can
speak His word to a distressed and disordered world.

III

Does this mean that the church must always be riding off
in all directions at once, and that its voice must always sound
like the hubbub of a crowd where everyone is shouting a different message at the same time, each man succeeding only
in making his neighbor unintelligible? Does it mean that the
church must be content to point out the wrongs in the common life, but never be able to make constructive suggestions
for their amendment? G. K. Chesterton was evidently op-
pressed with that sense of the futility of the church's efforts
to deal with social problems, when, after speaking at a meet-

ing of the Christian Social Union in Nottingham, he went home and wrote:

> "The Christian Social Union here
> Is very much annoyed;
> It seems there is some duty
> Which we never should avoid,
> And so they sing a lot of hymns
> To help the unemployed." [2]

But there are ways in which, without sacrificing any vital freedom, the influence of the Christian conscience can be brought to bear constructively upon the world which needs to be confronted with its challenge and to be restored by its hope and faith.

That influence can be mediated through a free pulpit. No pulpit is absolutely free, of course. A church which gives credentials to a minister has every right to expect him to be loyal to the terms on which he has accepted its ministry, and it has every right to expect him to seek service elsewhere if he cannot conscientiously maintain that loyalty. A congregation has every right to expect Christian courtesy, Christian humility, and Christian love in the pulpit. In times of heated controversy over political and social issues, when facts are hard to find and opinions are widely divided, it does not demand that the minister in the midst of his week's work should have been able to sift the truth, the whole truth, and nothing but the truth out of the cloud of rumours flying through the air and appearing in the press. Nor does it insist that when many good men disagree as to the solution of a social problem, the minister should on Saturday night have arrived at the final answer to the riddle for which a large part

[2] *Autobiography*, p. 167.

of the world is seeking. It is better if the minister does not attempt to do what his congregation does not ask of him. But that does not mean that social issues on which good men differ must be banished from the pulpit. How can they be, if the pulpit is true to the tradition of the prophets and to the spirit of Jesus? From beginning to end the Bible recognizes that the spiritual life of individuals and the social life of men are entangled one in the other, and that neither can be regarded as isolated from the other. A minister who preaches about the Christian life must preach about the difficult task of bringing the Christian ethic to bear upon every phase of human activity. When the pulpit has been most alive, it has dealt most frankly with the ethical needs of the common life. A student of the English church in the days before Tyndale has this to say about its preaching in that era:

"The message of the English pulpit, stored in a thousand manuscripts, bursts in upon us with an invigorating freshness. It reveals a Church striving by word of mouth, however fitfully, to curb wild passions and vicious habits, to educate the masses in a higher way of life, to reunite a discordant society in brotherly love and common service, to establish, according to its lights, a city of God upon the earth, in every home and community, warning, pleading, arguing, now with a show of learning, now with a quaint symbolism, now with threats, now with pathos, now with humour, a very human as well as a very formidable Church." [3]

Such forthright speech from the pulpit obviously constitutes a problem. It is a problem from the standpoint of those

[3] G. R. Owst, *Literature and Pulpit in Medieval England*, p. 14. Quoted by Rt. Rev. Hensley Henson, in Introduction to *Selected English Sermons*, pp. v, vi.

who would like to control the pulpit for their own purposes. In the time of the Tudor sovereigns of England what was called "tuning the pulpits" was a common practice, all the more valuable to the sovereigns because attendance at the parish churches was compulsory, and churchwardens "were required to report to the Bishop any political unsoundness or indication of doctrinal aberration." [4] Preaching on social issues is also a problem from the standpoint of the preacher. It may degenerate into mere secular discussion of politics and public affairs. Eighteenth-century preaching in Connecticut has sometimes been accused of having fallen into that pit. Abraham Bishop called the sermons of the day party harangues, "consisting of a little governor, a little of Congress, much of politics, and a very little of religion—a strange compote, like a carrot pie, having so little ingredients that the cook must christen it." [5] If the pulpit is to discuss social problems, it must do so from the standpoint of the Word of God, not as the agent of any secular group whatsoever, however idealistic such a group may be. If the church gives its ministers freedom to speak the truth as they see it, the church has a right to know that the pulpit has not yielded its freedom to any other control. Wise congregations want their ministers to have such freedom. They do not want to be told what they must think and do in every controversy, for they feel that they also have liberties to conserve. Dr. J. H. Oldham was right when he said: "It is not the function of the clergy to tell the laity how to act in public affairs, but rather to confront them with the Christian demand and to

[4] Hensley Henson, *Ibid.*, p. vii.
[5] Claude G. Bowers, *Jefferson and Hamilton*, p. 145.

encourage them to discover its application for themselves." [6]
But a congregation which is honestly seeking the kingdom
of God will want a minister who has convictions on matters
that are important to the social welfare. If he does not insist
that they must forfeit the name of Christian if they do not
think as he does, but respects their freedom in Christ as
sincerely as he wants them to respect his, they will want to
know at what conclusions he has arrived. If they know him
to be an honest, thoughtful man, whose mind is not a
museum of carefully labeled dogmas but is a workshop where
something constructive is being done, they will be helped
by knowing what he believes his Christian discipleship means
for him in certain situations in which conscientious people
are groping for light. Just as St. Paul felt that in some situations he could confidently interpret the Christian tradition
and in others knew that he was merely voicing his own
opinion,[7] so the minister must differentiate between the basic
convictions on which the Christian church is pretty well
agreed, and his own opinions on matters where the church is
not agreed. But if he uses his freedom wisely, and remem-
bers the Pauline interpretation of freedom, "though I be
free from all men, yet have I made myself servant unto all,"
he can, through the freedom of the pulpit, help in the process
of ploughing up and fertilizing and seeding the intellectual
soil out of which the mature convictions of the Christian
church on the problems of society grow and develop.

The influence of the Christian conscience can also be
brought to bear upon the world through experimental groups
within the church. Every denomination and every local con-

[6] *The Church and Its Function in Society*, p. 193.
[7] I Corinthians 7:6, 10.

gregation may well have within its organization groups that
are gathered together around special interests, studying and
working at particular problems in the relationship of Christianity to life. The church member who objects to a pronounce-
ment made in the name of his denomination or his congregation by some church meeting, on the ground that when he
joined the church he did not do so with the understanding
that the church by majority votes could speak for him on labor
policies or international questions, has a sound argument. But
he does not object if some group within the church which
has been giving thoughtful consideration to some social
problem in the light of Christian teaching, goes to work to
try to carry out into practical reality the convictions at which
the group has arrived, so long as it does not commit the whole
church to views which the whole church does not hold. It is
a sign of healthy democracy in the church when in a single
congregation there are different groups working on opposite
sides when questions of moment are in the air, so long as
mutual respect and good will are maintained within the
Christian fellowship. Such differences put a strain on Christian grace, but what is Christian grace for if not to be strained
by the tensions which are the inevitable concomitants of
vigorous minds and wills acting under the compulsions of
conscience?

Out of the church's thought and life, stimulated by the
exercise of Christian liberty in the pulpit and the pew, there
emerge from time to time great basic agreements which with
a reasonable degree of accuracy can be designated as the convictions of the Christian church on certain social questions.
The meeting of minds and the sharing of life out of which
these agreements come are among the ways in which God

speaks His word to and through His church. Such agreements do not come so frequently or so easily as we sometimes wish, but they do come, and their coming is one of the evidences of the pressure of God's life upon responsive human life. There is always an element of mystery in the whole transaction. Sometimes the common mind is reached with a suddenness which is wholly unexpected and startling. Washington Gladden said of the crystallization of the anti-slavery conviction which took place just before the election of Lincoln as President:

"No man could help seeing that this political revolution registered an ethical advance in the American people. There had come about, during the eight years, a change in the moral feelings of the multitude. Their ideals had been, in some good measure, transformed. . . . Such changes as these in the habitual thoughts of people, in their ruling ideas are to be looked for; the hope of the world is in them. The notion that human nature is a fixed quantity is sufficiently absurd, on the face of it; but such a transformation of the moral feelings of a whole population as occurred in the eight years of which we are speaking ought to put an end to all such pessimistic reasoning." [8] Even more significant is his comment on the rapidity with which that change took place: "It is interesting now," he wrote in his latter years, "to recall the growth of the anti-slavery sentiment. The rapidity of this movement was something phenomenal. I am sure that no one thought so then: we all felt that the mills of the gods were grinding as slowly as is their wont; we were often crying out 'How long, O Lord, how long!' But we can see now, when we look back

[8] *Recollections*, p. 95.

and count the years, that opinion was moving forward at a prodigious speed." [9]

Washington Gladden was speaking of a change which took place in the thinking of the nation. But that sort of changed mind also takes place within the church as events compel Christian people to ask how their loyalty to Christ ought to be expressed in specific situations. Part of the genius of preaching is to recognize when such tidal movements of opinion are taking place and to interpret to people what has been taking place unconsciously in their own minds under the influence of God. A preacher knows that he has done this when someone says, "You have said something that has been in the back of my mind for a long time, but I couldn't put it into words." That is no mean service. When a gathering like the Conference on Life and Work at Oxford in 1937 speaks for equality of opportunity for all races, for the exaltation of human rights above pre-occupations with property in a commercialized civilization, brands war as sin, and pleads for a united church to serve a closely inter-related world, it is expressing convictions which have been crystallizing in the mind of the church until they can fairly be put forward as the message of the church to our day. The temptation of such gatherings is on the one hand that they will run far out beyond the actual mind of the church, causing confusion by assuming positions which only a minority in the churches actually hold, and, on the other hand, that they will timidly fall far behind the moving mind of the church, fearing to express convictions that the people in the churches really want to have proclaimed in their name. There is no infallible measuring rod in these matters. The

[9] *Ibid.*, p. 46.

church is blessed when it has leaders who are wise enough
and sensitive enough to be able intuitively to apprehend the
spirit that is moving the hearts of Christian people as they
confront the needs of the world. Both in such formal expressions and through the informal ways in which the church
touches the world, these basic agreements of Christian people
on the human problems of the world exert a profound influence.

It is of the utmost importance that the Christian church
should never abdicate its position of influence upon the social
life of the world. It has been characteristic of the churches
of the English-speaking regions that they have felt keenly
their responsibility for "Christianizing the social order," to
use the phrase of Walter Rauschenbusch, which is still a
great phrase for a great cause. This has been true in part because the churches of the English-speaking countries have
existed in an atmosphere of political liberty which has made
it possible for them to be socially creative forces. Continental
theology has tended to think of the church as an order quite
distinct from the family and the state, and out of its sphere
when venturing into the field of social ethics, where it is
believed that God the Wholly Other must intervene when in
His wisdom He wills change, while the church waits and
worships in faithful expectancy. It is not unfair to remember
that this passive theology with its distrust of activism, has
become influential during years of bitter disappointment and
disillusionment with the results of what used to be called
progress, and that it spread out from regions where political
conditions made it impossible for the church to exert much
direct influence upon social life, except at the point of crisis

where the church felt called upon to stand in revolt against
the state, as it has most gloriously done. We have much to
learn from those who will make no compromise in their
doctrine of the majesty of God, who build their ultimate
hopes not on the broken reed of man's genius but on the
good will of God, and who are sure that salvation lies in
hearing and obeying the Word of God. We who have talked
glibly about being up and doing with a heart for any fate
have never known emotionally how terrible the fate of man
in this world can be until now. We need to be reminded that
it is God that sitteth upon the circle of the earth, and that
we are His feeble creatures. Nevertheless, it may be that
the activist faith of the English-speaking peoples, and of
like-minded Christians in many lands, including the Orient,
has been given to the world for such a time as this. There
are two windows in St. Paul's great admonition, "Work out
your own salvation with fear and trembling, for it is God that
worketh in you both to will and to do of His good pleasure." [10]
One window is toward the heavenly places, where God wills
and does of His good pleasure. The other opens on the
world where human beings like ourselves must with fear and
trembling grapple with the social ills of a very sick world, in
the faith that whatever power we have to build a better world
is the power of God working in us.

In Emerson's *Journal* there is the record of a day in 1827
when the Concord philosopher, then still in the Unitarian
ministry, was attending a meeting of the Bible Society in
St. Augustine, Florida. Through a blunder in manage-
ment, the meeting was held in an upstairs room of the
government house, overlooking a square where slaves were

[10] Philippians 2:12-13.

being auctioned off while the Bible Society was in session. The windows were open to let in the sunshine, and they also let in the voice of the auctioneer. Emerson's comment was: "One ear therefore heard the glad tidings of great joy, whilst the other was regaled with 'Going, gentlemen, going.' And almost without changing our position we might aid in sending the Scriptures into Africa, or bid for 'four children without the mother' who had been kidnapped therefrom." [11] The sounds from the slave market were no doubt disconcerting to the Bible Society, and yet salutary. The church cannot close its ears to the cries of race and clan while it listens for the Word of God, for the Word of God comes to the church's ears through the bitter needs of men as well as through the Bible. The church must preach the gospel as it comes to us through the Bible, and it must also bring its influence to bear upon the places where men are bought and sold. Churches which have enjoyed the priceless privilege of carrying on their work under the institutions of political freedom have, because of their heritage, a special responsibility to relate their gospel to the world.

IV

That world as it confronts us today is a world at war. Its need for the Word of God was never more clearly recognized by all sorts and kinds of people, who are saying as William Rose Benét said in some recent verses:

"There are words
like *blood* and *sweat* and *tears*, as now we know—
simple old words like *bravery*, *faith*, and *death*,

[11] Bliss Perry (ed.), *The Heart of Emerson's Journals*, p. 36.

> plain words like *horror* and *pain* and *loss* and *grief,*
> and a word we somewhere heard but long forgot
> or just mislaid—the Word they said was God. . . ." [12]

The responsibility upon the shoulders of the preacher was never greater than now, when the spiritual poverty of a shattered world is writ large across the sky where the searchlights peer by night for the death-dealing bomber, when the voice of the commentator with war news is never silent, nor dies the strain of human grief away. The wide and, alas, too often bitter differences of opinion as to what is the Word of God for this hour indicate that the task of the preacher in a world at war is not a simple one.

It must be remembered that the minister faces a twofold obligation as he encounters the issues which war forces upon the Christian conscience. For one thing, he faces the decisions which he must make for himself as an individual Christian. Like everyone else, he is responsible to God for what he does and says and is when the future of the world is in the balance. But beyond the personal decisions which he must make, he also faces decisions as a leader in the church. The church is responsible to God for what it does and says and is as a Christian fellowship when the future of the world is in the balance. Every minister helps to determine the rôle which the church plays in a time of war. Both of these obligations press home on the minister with relentless urgency. They cannot be evaded, for evasion itself is a decision.

As an individual Christian, the minister must try to see the moral issues of the conflict clearly. Here he immediately runs full-tilt into the saying recorded in the Sermon on the

[12] William Rose Benét, "To Ideologists," in *Saturday Review of Literature;* Feb. 28, 1942.

Mount, "Judge not, that ye be not judged." That saying may be so interpreted as to create a flabby mind blind to all differences between good and bad, or, as is more commonly the case in a world where untainted good and unrelieved bad are hard to find, between better and worse. This flabby mind usually appears in the guise of "seeing both sides of the question." But seeing both sides of the question ought not to mean a state of perpetual intellectual suspense. The purpose of seeing both sides is to have an accurate basis for the decisiveness of mind which is essential to all constructive effort. Did Jesus himself remain in a state of suspense with regard to the moral failures of the Pharisees? He said frankly that the Pharisees tithed mint, anise and cummin and neglected justice, mercy, and faith. He recognized that Peter and James and John had their moral limitations, but when the pressing problem was the sin of the Pharisees, he met that issue without evasion or circumlocution. It would be a sad thing if loyalty to Jesus necessitated the obliteration of moral discriminations in our view of the contemporary world. There is a saying attributed to Jesus in John's Gospel, which needs to be put alongside the sweeping prohibition of moral judgments which seems to be implied by the saying in Matthew. "I judge no man," so he begins in the Fourth Gospel. "And yet" (was that perhaps too sweeping a statement?), "if I judge, my judgment is true; for I am not alone, but I and the Father that sent me." [13] He could not avoid differentiating between the Beloved Disciple and Herod. Too many far-reaching interests were at stake in that difference. But he did not judge Herod on the basis of personal whim or private prejudice. He made his judgment in the

[13] John 8:15-16.

light of his unique knowledge of the will and character of God. There was no hard censoriousness in his judgments. He recognized, we may be sure, that the evil in Herod was not the whole man. Every man is a mixture of good and bad. No doubt he took into consideration the influences which had made Herod what he was. He blazed out in indignation against wrongs committed by people in power, but there is no record of his hating any people. No one seems ever to have gone beyond the point where Jesus was still trying to help him become the man God meant him to be. He showed that there is no ultimate contradiction between judgment and love, but that the only judgment which is just is one permeated with good will, while the only loving judgment is one founded on justice. And yet he saw moral issues clearly, and did not blink the fact that moral issues are never abstractions, but are always revealed in the actions of people. The minister who is trying as an individual to be a follower of Jesus will not see the moral issues in the present war with the unerring clarity that Jesus would see them. But that does not absolve him from his responsibility to see them as clearly as he can.

V

As a Christian individual he cannot remain in a state of suspense on the question of pacifism, which the events of our time thrust home to every active conscience. He cannot decide that question for the whole church, but he must decide it for himself. If the problem of a Christian's participation in war has never given him a pain in the mind, or if he has forgotten that he ever wrestled with it, he is in a morally perilous predicament, which like all moral predicaments is all the more perilous if he is not aware of it. If he feels morally superior to people who have arrived at a conclusion which differs from his own, he is not likely to be a constructive leader of the church in the midst of a world at war. If he has not clarified in his own mind the basis on which he makes his decision, he is not apt to have a clear-cut conviction on this matter.

A Christian cannot determine his attitude toward the ethical problem of war on the basis of the issues of the present conflict, although the flames of this struggle light up the principles that are involved, and make them stand out with a sharpness that they do not have when they are considered as abstractions. No man ought to be afraid to rethink and perhaps restate his convictions after he has seen them against the background which the world now presents. A Christian cannot determine his position on this question by balancing New Testament passages against each other, or by any legalistic interpretation of particular sayings of Jesus. If in other realms of conduct, Jesus was careful not to replace the Pharisaic code with a new set of regulations, it would seem reasonable to suppose that he made no exception in this troubled area. A Christian cannot determine his answer to this question on the basis of what he can imagine Jesus as doing. We do not know what Jesus would do were he an American citizen today, and the political attitudes which he seems to have assumed as an inhabitant of a province which had been conquered by the ruling Empire of the day do not constitute a pattern for the political attitudes of the citizens of a country which still has the freedom and the responsibilities of the United States of America.

There is, however, a twofold basis on which a Christian's

decision as to his duty in time of war may legitimately
be founded. He must decide what course of action in
the tangled political situation of the contemporary world
seems to him best to express the spirit which Jesus expressed
in his day, for which we have no better name than the
spirit of love. (In so doing, he must consider how he can
express good will not only toward the individuals with
whom he may have first-hand encounters, but also toward
multitudes of other individuals whom he will never know
personally but who will be vitally affected by the decision made by him and by other people in like case with himself.) He must also decide what course of action will lead
toward the kind of a world in which people can more completely express the spirit of Jesus than any man can today
when every man is involved with his fellows in corporate
contradictions of the spirit of Jesus in the economic and
political systems under which we live. (This obligation cannot be brushed aside by saying that it is an attempt to let
the end justify the means. It would be truer to say that it is
an attempt to appraise the validity of an action in the light
of its future consequences. No man who cares about his
fellow-creatures with a concern which has any spiritual kinship with that of Jesus can ignore the consequences to them
of what he may do in critical situations.)

On this twofold basis, most Christians will not refuse to
participate in war when they have reluctantly been driven to
the conclusion that such refusal may make their fellow-men
the victims of outrageous wrong. Many have tried to find
some line that can be drawn between the use of military power
for police purposes and the use of military power in war, but it
has been an unsuccessful search. The means employed are the

same in either case, or may be the same if enough people are in revolt against the authority exercising the police power. If we are ever to have an orderly world in which even rough justice can obtain, we must have an international authority with force at its disposal for the maintenance of peace and the exercise of justice. I once believed, along with many others, that the agencies of international justice could dispense with military power and could rely upon reason and the moral force of justice itself to hold the world together. The facts of contemporary history make it impossible now to believe in the efficacy of international law divorced from any power of enforcement. If the use of military and naval power by international agencies is legitimate, and can be the best available expression of deep concern for human welfare in the modern world, then it would seem that a Christian may use such force to help create the conditions under which the world can have such international agencies. Few people to-day have any illusions about war. War cannot create a world in which order and freedom, justice and mercy, brotherhood and the good life are possible. That world must be built in the spirits of men. But in desperate times like our own, participation in a war which should never have happened may be the only way of preventing the political tyranny under which it would be impossible even to work for a decent world. Without the military defeat of the Axis powers, we cannot have freedom even to attempt the establishment of a free fellowship of free nations. Every Christian man must settle this problem for himself, maintaining his fellowship with and respect for those who hold a different view. If he is a minister, his congregation have a right to know how he in

his own conscience conceives his course of action when his
country is at war.

VI

As a Christian individual, however, he cannot stop with the
definition of his formal relationship with the war activity in
which his country is engaged. He has other personal relationships with the war in addition to those which involve
his attitude toward the cause to which his government is
committed. He is concerned with the Word of God which
is our hope for a redeemed earth, a Word which must be
heard through all the din of world-encircling battles. There
is a Voice even now telling us to be penitent as we confess
our share in the universal selfishness that found its logical
conclusion in universal conflict. There is a Voice that bids
us acknowledge the right of other men to the freedom that
we want for ourselves, and that reminds us that the ultimate
source of freedom is obedience to God. There is a Voice
warning us that hatred destroys the very treasures of the spirit
that we are concerned to defend, that revenge is itself spiritual
defeat, and that as Christians we face the difficult task of
standing against what we believe to be hideous wrong and at
the same time of preserving the spiritual integrity for the
sake of which we oppose wrong. There is a Voice calling to
us through all the sufferings of the world, inviting us into a
fellowship of burden-bearing and promising us that as we
practice sacrificial generosity on behalf of the homeless and
the hungry and the stricken, we can even now be laying
spiritual foundations for the world that is to be. There is a
Voice urging us to think, to learn, to plan, and to work now
for a new kind of peace to follow this war, so that we may

be ready to make the beginnings of a really new order, in which there shall be impartial law, economic opportunity, and political fellowship for all nations. There is a Voice that speaks through the silence of the human spirit, in response to which we are moved to pray, not because we can altogether understand how our prayers can help to right the world, but because, believing that there is a Creative Will involved with us in all this tragedy and pain, we cannot hold our peace, but must lay at the feet of God our deep concerns for this world, which is not our world but His. There is a Voice that challenges us to keep faith with that Mighty God, trusting that into whatsoever darkness we may descend, He keeps faith with us. Just because he is a Christian man, the minister has his own personal response to make to these and many other obligations which God lays upon his conscience in this time of war.

VII

The minister also faces peculiar responsibilities as a leader in the church when the nation is at war. The individual views of the minister may not be the views of all the members of the church which he serves, or even of a majority. While exercising the liberty of a Christian conscience, it is not for him to speak as the representative of the whole church on matters where he obviously is not representative. It is not for him explicitly or by implication to read out of the church those whose considered judgments on the issues before the nation differ from his. Neither is it his duty or privilege to make them so uncomfortable in the church that they will exercise the inalienable right of every American churchman and absent themselves from the church. When great issues are at stake and feelings run high it is not easy for the minister to be true to his own convictions and also true to the spirit of fellowship in the church which he serves. His success in maintaining both personal honesty and Christian fellowship will depend not so much on what he does or says during the crisis as on how he has done and said things before the crisis. If people believe in him and know that he believes in them, the strains produced by differing views can be used to strengthen rather than weaken the bonds that unite pastor and people. If there is suspicion or lack of confidence on either side, the crisis will surely reveal it.

VIII

It is not the task of the minister, however, merely to hold a church together through a time of war. He is to lead the church so that the church as a Christian fellowship can mediate the Word of God which can be the healing of the world's ills. How shall he exercise that leadership?

He can help the people of the church to see the war in perspective. There has been much discussion as to whether or not ministers should preach about the war. One of the polls of public opinion reported a majority of its correspondents as opposed to pulpit comments on the war, on the ground that people come to church to get away from the conflict. If that means that ministers should not attempt to be news commentators, well and good. This age of radio and streamlined journalism is amply supplied with them. If that means that people do not want to hear about the war all the time, it reveals a sound instinct on the part of the people. But no one today can get away from the war, even in church. It is there, whether we speak of it or not. It is the background of all that we think and plan and do. But it is not the ultimate background. It is the function of the church to try to see the war against the background of the purposes of God, who is Himself afflicted in all the afflictions of His children, who has shown us in Christ His intentions for human life, who is the Lord of heaven and earth before wars began and after the last gun has been fired, who is the Upholder of those who make it their supreme purpose to work with Him for a kingdom of righteousness and love. A preacher may or may not mention the war explicitly, but he has missed his unique opportunity if people go out from church without seeing the war in which they are deeply involved against that horizon. Who is going to sketch that final and eternal background until it is unmistakably clear before the minds of men if the preacher does not do it? How shall we see the issues of this awesome era truly except as we are reminded week in and week out that God still lives?

IX

The minister can also exercise his leadership in keeping the church hospitable to varied points of view with regard to the issues which the war raises. A Christian church is a fellowship around one central loyalty to Christ. United in that loyalty, members of Christ's church must trust each other and believe in each other, even when they differ widely in their interpretation of their Christian duty. There is room in the church for pacifist and non-pacifist, for adherents of various plans for post-war reconstruction, and for people who appraise at different valuations the British Empire and the U.S.S.R. and the Congress Party in India. There is no room in the church for hatred and prejudice and the assumption of

omniscience. If the church is to help with the world (where
differing opinions on political questions will always be hotly
held) it must give a demonstration of the power of the grace
of God to enable people to "agree to differ but resolve to
love," [14] to use a phrase contributed to the Christian cause
by a Chinese Christian leader. John Morley once remonstrated with J. S. Mill's radical friends who were angry with
him for loving Wordsworth who was no longer with them
on political questions. "Wordsworth is against you no doubt
in the battle you are now waging," said John Morley, "but
after you have won, the world will need more than ever
those qualities which Wordsworth is keeping alive and
flourishing." [15] Without underestimating the crucial character of the questions that will be decided by the outcome of
the war, can it not truthfully be said that when the war is
over the world will need all the Christian capital that has
been conserved in any group of Christians, and that it is part
of the minister's task to keep the Christian spirit alive and
flourishing in the midst of the church's diversity of political
opinions?

X

As a leader in the church, the minister must also help to
make the church a fellowship of compassion. In time of
war the tide of suffering rises so high that it is easy to persuade
one's self that nothing can be done about it. The mass of
suffering is so great that it easily loses its personal character.
(As a matter of fact, we dare not personalize it too much, lest

[14] Dr. Timothy T. Liu, Dean of Theological Department, Yen-
ching University.
[15] *Recollections*, Vol. I, p. 67.

it overwhelm us.) The tale of the world's suffering is re-
peated so steadily in each day's news that our feelings with
regard to it become blunted. Perhaps it is God's mercy that
our feelings do lose their extreme sensitivity, or our own
vicarious suffering might cripple all our powers of usefulness.
John Brown said of the doctor in *Rab and His Friends* that
though pity had ceased to be an emotion with him, it had
become a motive.[16] That is a translation which all people
must make who are to live helpfully in the midst of world-
wide suffering. The peril of the world is that it may lose
the spirit of compassion both as emotion and motive. The
peril of the church is that it may stimulate an emotional
compassion which never becomes the driving motive power
of action. The responsibility of the church is to make sure that
as the emotion of pity loses its acuteness, it takes a new form
as efficient, persistent, courageous, generous activity for the
relief of refugees and prisoners and for persecuted, wounded,
homeless, hungry, needy people wherever that is possible.
There may be disagreements in the church as to the limits of
possibility, but there are no disagreements as to the obligation laid upon those who bear the name of Christ. In this
ministry of compassion, the minister must show the way.

If compassion is to be the motive of effective action, the
minister must keep alive the church's interest and faith in
endeavors to establish an international order which can deal
at their source with the causes of war. In May, 1917,
Ambassador Walter Hines Page wrote a letter to President
Wilson, describing the sights at a war hospital next door to
his house in London: "God pity us for not having organized
the world better than this. We'll do it yet, Mr. President—

16 *Rab and His Friends*, p. 18.

you'll do it: and thank God for you. If we do not organize
Europe and make another catastrophe impossible, life will
not be worth being born into except to the few whose
days happen to fall between recurring devastations of the
world." [17] It was not done. The task remains still before us.
It may be more difficult than ever after this war. But even
while we are in the midst of the conflict we need to remember
that the right to have an international society, not a world
ruled by a master race, is one of the goals for which we are
contending. Without setting himself up as an expert in international affairs, a minister who takes seriously the New Testament hope of the kingdom of God can with a ready heart
help to lead the way toward a community of nations, and
can help to prepare the people of the Christian churches for
the sacrifices which the creation of such community will
entail.

Here, however, the minister's primary task is to interpret
the Christian basis for such community. The Christian
church feels the need for a political organization of nations
under international law because the Christian church believes that mankind is one family under the Fatherhood of
God under whose Providence all nations exist. The most
tragic aspect of international war is that it is a disruption of
the family of mankind, during which the ordinary expressions of a fraternal relationship are cut off. It is the privilege
of the Christian church to keep stressing that family bond
until such time as we can renew the normal relationships of
the children of God. During the American Civil War, Dr.
Horace Furness, who later edited the Variorum Shakespeare,

[17] Burton J. Hendrick, *Life and Letters of Walter H. Page*, Vol.
II, p. 263.

served with those who tended the wounded at Fredericksburg. He was in the railroad station one day when President
Lincoln entrained there after a visit to the Union Army.
Opposite the station was a factory, which was in use as a
hospital, and, as the President boarded his train, the windows
of the factory were crowded with wounded men watching
him. He went immediately to the rear platform to address
them. Said Dr. Furness in a letter, they were anxious for
a stirring address, but Mr. Lincoln merely reminded them
that their enemies were their "brothers in error" and that
after the war had ended their children and grandchildren
would have to live together with those from the South for
many generations. The crowd was very much disappointed.[18]
But is not that authentic Christianity? When this war is
over, the children of men must go on living on a very small
planet, and while we can make no peace with oppression, we
must keep alive the conviction that we are all one family
under God.

XI

To this end, the minister must keep his people informed
concerning the ecumenical church, and consciously identified with it. While we wait for the establishment of political
fellowship among the nations, and for the completion of
federation among all the churches, of which happily we already have the beginnings, we now have a spiritual fellowship among the Christian churches of the world which we
must not allow the war to dissipate. Beneath the political
differences that divide us, beneath the battles that engage us,

[18] *The Letters of Horace Howard Furness*, edited by H. H. F. J.,
Vol. I, p. 114.

beneath all the troubles that seem to overwhelm us, there is a deep unity of heart among Christians in every nation which we must not give up. Was there ever a time when so many individual Christians had so many deep personal friendships across international lines? Was there ever a time since the divisions of Christendom began when there had been set in motion so many cooperative undertakings in the name of the universal Christian church? When, since New Testament days, was a more genuinely Christian epistle written than that sent to the churches of this country by the Christian leaders of Japan who visited this country a year ago? "Dear Comrades in Christ! Greetings!" they began, and they ended: "The world situation grows increasingly ominous. No matter what turn things may take, however, we shall always treasure the friendship and fellowship which made our conferences and contacts so delightful and meaningful. Let us maintain the soul fellowship which is centered in Christ and bind our two nations together with a bond of unceasing and earnest prayer." [19] No political organization can ever hold the world together unless there is a spiritual unity at the heart of it. May not the minister help to build that inner unity if he can lead a church into a deeper fellowship of spirit with the universal church of Christ?

XII

In 1863 the then United States Minister to the Netherlands, James S. Pike, finding himself in London, went to call upon Thomas Carlyle. He came away saying that Carlyle "seemed to believe that there is a God, but that the Devil is

[19] *Federal Council Bulletin*, December, 1941.

more than a match for Him." [20]   The preacher of the Word
of God must proclaim to a world well acquainted with the
powers of evil the God who is more than a match for the
world rulers of this darkness. Without minimizing or con-
cealing the evil that now is, he must proclaim that the day of
the Lord is not darkness but light. As T. S. Eliot puts the
Word upon the lips of the Church,

> "There shall always be the Church and the World
>   And the Heart of Man
>   Shivering and fluttering between them, choosing
>   and chosen,
>   Valiant, ignoble, dark and full of light
>   Swinging between Hell Gate and Heaven Gate.
>   And the Gates of Hell shall not prevail.
>   Darkness now, then
>   Light,
>   Light." [21]

[20] *Atlantic Monthly*, December, 1939.

[21] *The Rock*, pp. 47-8, by permission of Harcourt, Brace and Co.,
Inc., publishers.

IV

THE WORD OF GOD FOR EVERY MAN

"As every man hath received the gift, even so minister the same one to another, as good stewards of the manifold grace of God."

I PETER 4:10.

THE WORD OF GOD FOR EVERY MAN

T HE Master of one of the Yale colleges observed after a Sunday service in Battell Chapel: "Preaching is like shooting quail. If you aim for all the birds, you hit none, but if you aim for one, you are likely to get several." He was right, and he put his finger on one of the elements which distinguishes preaching from other forms of public speech. A lecturer may address an audience, but the preacher speaks to a man. It is one of the problems of preaching that it must be public speech with a private significance. The preacher speaks to a group of people, and yet the effectiveness of his preaching depends upon the degree to which each hearer feels that the message is for him as an individual. One of the perils of preaching is that the preacher may be tempted to use methods unworthy of his calling in his desire to establish this rapport with each of his hearers. The stage has its tricks, known to every skilful actor, by which a subtle relationship is established between the man on the stage and the man in the audience. But the pulpit is not a stage, and the preacher is not an actor, and a congregation is not an audience. When the message of the pulpit fails to ring true, sometimes it is because these necessary distinctions have been forgotten. The relationship between the preacher and the man in the pew is in quite a different realm. It is inherent in the very nature of the gospel which is the substance of Christian preaching. For though that gospel has its application to all the broad sweep of hu-

man life, its main concern is with the individuals who make
up the corporate life of mankind, who are vitally affected at
the core of their spiritual beings by that corporate life, and
who vitally affect one another through the organized expression of their wills and desires. When the man in the pew feels
that, so far as the preacher is concerned, he has been lost
in the crowd, something is wrong with that preacher's interpretation of the gospel. Whether the preacher be discussing
the Creation, or the labor problem, or "the heart's meeting
with the wonders of the life divine," [1] he can never afford to
forget that he is called to "present every man perfect in
Christ," and that whatever truth he has to convey must find
lodgement not in the mass-mind but in the minds of particular people.

It is a basic conviction of the Christian faith that not
only has God spoken a Word about man, his nature, his
need, and his destiny, but that He is speaking a Word in
our time to every man. It has been a strange paradox that
during the years when political democracy has been seeking
to foster and to develop the dignity of the individual, certain
aspects of scientific truth have seemed to indicate that the
individual is an insignificant pigmy swept along by forces so
vast that he has little chance to determine to any degree his
own destiny, and economic units have become so great and
so impersonal that the individual has become lost and forgotten in their large, relentless operations. It is not to be
wondered at that political democracy should at last be faced
with the necessity of justifying itself at the bar of reason
and even of defending itself on the field of battle. The
Christian faith that God is concerned with every man sounds

[1] A. V. G. Allen, *Life and Letters of Phillips Brooks*, Vol. I, p. 253.

to some modern folk like the far off echo of a world long lost, and it comes to others as the main hope for the recovery of a quality of life without which the world will always be poor, if it can exist as a civilized world at all. The preacher of the Word of God must bring to every hearer not only the conviction that God has a message to the world but also the assurance that God has a word for him as an individual.

That Word begins with the elemental fact that life counts for something. Every preacher confronts many people who have been through so many shocks and dislocations that they are on the verge of the greatest of all dislocations, the fear that their very existence has no significance. A man can endure almost anything except the sense that what he is going through has no meaning, and that in every attempt to make his life count he is frustrated at the outset because his life was never intended to mean anything. As Dostoievsky made the Grand Inquisitor say in *The Brothers Karamazov*: "The secret of man's being is not only to live but to have something to live for." [2]

When difficulties mount, as they have mounted for everyone in recent years, the amount of energy with which they are met depends to a great extent upon the background against which they are seen. "We have to deal with a pestilence of the soul," says Franz Werfel. "A consistently godless world is like a picture without perspective. Without perspective everything is meaningless, and when everything is without meaning our natural human rights have no meaning either. Our souls refuse to believe any longer in their indestructibility and hence in their eternal responsibility. Since he [modern man] is unable to believe in any kind of

[2] Book V, Chap. 5.

indestructibility he already acknowledges the Devil's creed. For him everything is fleeting, and nothing is permanent. . . ." [3]

For people who face the frustrations which are involved in modern life, there is much that the techniques of the psychiatrist and the social worker can do to make them more adequate for life. A minister should by all means know what resources his community provides to help people make their adjustments to a chaotic and bewildering world. Unless he has had unusual opportunities for training, he is ill advised if he attempts to use psychiatric methods himself. He has no excuse if he has not done enough reading in the field of mental hygiene so that he knows what the most common problems are and how they are recognized. But the minister's main contribution is not in that field at all. The unique contribution which he can make is to restore faith in the significance of life in its totality by helping struggling men and women to see their problems in their perspective against the purposes of God.

II

This sense of frustration, which is found among people of all ages in times of great uncertainty, is especially acute among young people. It shows itself in a variety of ways. Sometimes it takes the form of bravado, an outward defiance of custom, tradition, and the things held sacred by an older generation. Sometimes it shows itself as a craving for authority. It is from the ranks of youth that the most devoted followers are recruited for almost any leader who comes forward with a dynamic program which he represents without reservation

[3] *Embezzled Heaven,* p. 423.

as the panacea for the world's ills. Sometimes youth's sense of frustration appears in a strenuous denial of the validity of moral judgments. "There isn't religion for our genera‧ tion, as there used to be—I mean a quite certain, helping religion that explained and alleviated a little," the heroine of a modern novel says to her father. "When you haven't any religion or any—well, real ideals to live for, there isn't any absolute wrong, Daddy. Just small mistakes and successes." [4] It is not only in novels that such moral nihilism is expressed. Sometimes the underlying sense of futility results in a hard and determined attempt to seize what transitory satisfactions can be had in material possessions and material power, pursued with cynical disregard of any more lasting values.

There is nothing new about the problem of relating youth to religion. In 1744, "addressing his remarks to the gallery" of the church in Northampton, Jonathan Edwards said to those gathered there: "I dare appeal to those young people that have in great measure neglected religion and given the reins to their inclination and spent a great Deal of their time over wine, mirth and those Diversions that are inconsistent with a serious Religion." [5] If the preacher today does not address youth in those terms, it is in part because those who have neglected religion are not within hearing distance. And yet the vitality of religious movements among students, the enthusiasm of the multitudes who attend summer conferences for youth and the seriousness with which young people almost anywhere will embark upon religious discussions all indicate that the very uncertainties which produce a feeling of bafflement also produce a hunger for the Word of

[4] Sylvia Thompson, *Hounds of Spring*, p. 157.
[5] Ola E. Winslow, *Jonathan Edwards*, p. 228.

God. It is to this hunger that we preachers must learn how to speak. For there is a Word of God to this generation, reminding us that there are moral foundations on which all satisfying life must be built, assuring us that there are spiritual resources adequate for the most confused and challenging times, calling us to forget ourselves in a great purpose to work with the creative forces that are able to fashion a better life for men, and revealing to us in Christ the Way, the Truth, and the Life for every generation.

I would hazard the guess that a great deal of preaching to young people misses the mark because the preacher in his effort to catch the interest of youth stays on the periphery of the gospel instead of going to the heart of it. What youth needs from the church is not entertainment but religion, and nothing is so interesting to young people as religion when it is related to the actual needs of life. Last summer the *British Weekly* published a letter from a soldier in an anti-aircraft unit describing some of his experiences in church-going. He concluded:

"If I were asked the reason for the coldness in so many of our churches, I should say one, and probably a very important reason is this, so often it is the 'gospel of Democracy' that is preached and not the 'Good News of the Kingdom.' I can recall many times when I have sat in strange churches and listened to an exaltation of the moral goodness of democracy at large and the British Empire in particular. It may help and inspire some folk, but it leaves me empty. I come away wondering what God has been trying to say to me. . . . When I go to church I want to leave the world and join the fellowship of Saints, Angels, Martyrs and the whole glorious company who are worshipping and adoring Jesus—the Lord

Jesus. I want to hear a sermon about Him, not about Hitler. I want to thrill and feast my soul on the Glory of His coming kingdom, not the New World Order to be run by the U.S.A. and the British Empire." [6] That young man may have failed to see as clearly as he should the logical connection between the religion of Jesus and a world order of free men. But he was right in his instinctive desire to find in the church a message that centered in Christ.

"Youth is a terrible thing; it can be used to build heaven or hell," said Ramsay MacDonald at Glasgow in 1924. Whether the energies of youth are used to create a paradise or an inferno depends in large part upon the fellowships in which youth is bound up. William James's dictum that "the difference between a good man and a bad one is the choice of the cause" [7] is nowhere so true as among young men and women, who have most to give to the causes with which they are identified. Young people, even more than those who are older, are moulded and colored by the mind and purposes of their groups. "When young people violate sacred family traditions and smile complacently," Miriam Van Waters has written, "with no loss of self-esteem, it is not because they have become anti-social; it indicates probably that they dwell in some other island of social-culture which smiles upon their activities, and which is endorsed by some powerful group of adults." [8] It is equally true that when young people violate mediocre family traditions, and to the astonishment of their elders embark on adventurous attempts to end ancient in-

[6] Issue of August 21, 1941.
[7] *Letters of William James*, edited by his son, Henry James. Vol. II, p. 28.
[8] *Youth in Conflict*, p. 128.

justices and to create a better society, it probably indicates
that they have found their setting in some fellowship outside
their homes which has a more intense spirit of altruism than
their homes have. The Christian gospel, therefore, cannot
be adequately interpreted to youth without some correlative
interpretation of the church as the body of Christ, the fellowship in which the individual Christian is rooted, from which
he draws life, and through which he serves. The potentialities of youth will never be realized among isolated individuals
seeking truth and creating good. Only in the fellowship of
the church can those potentialities find their fullest realization. The preaching of Christian truth is incomplete so long
as it leaves the individual seeker for the Christian life cut off
from the church which has been the historic Christian fellowship. The preacher who would help young people to overcome the sense of frustration which is inseparable from an
exaggerated individualism, must link with the challenge of
the Christian ethic and the support of the Christian faith a
convincing interpretation of the necessity of the Christian
church.

III

The gospel that every man's life counts for something
grows out of the Christian faith that every man has worth
in the sight of God. In Henry James's *Portrait of a Lady*,
Ralph Touchett says of Lord Warburton, "He has ceased to
believe in himself, and he doesn't know what to believe in."
If it is true that a man who believes in nothing but himself
may find himself in the end with nothing at all to believe in,
it is equally true that faith in the God and Father of Jesus
Christ creates a corresponding faith in the incalculable value

of every individual. It is the conviction that every individual is dear to God who is the Father of all men that enables a man to believe in himself without becoming a mere egotist. Augustine said with insight in his *Confessions*: "What I do know of myself I know by Thy shining upon me." [9]

The view of life which we call democracy is not identical with Christianity, but the two have much in common, and the basic confidence in the worth of the individual man which democracy represents finds one of its strongest bulwarks in the Christian faith that every man is valuable in the sight of God. It is that faith for which the world gropes when colossal and tragic events shake the individual's confidence that it makes any difference what he is or what he does. The preacher must proclaim in season and out of season the Christian faith that every man's life finds its deepest meaning in its relationship with God, to whom every soul has a worth not calculable in human mathematics.

IV

The Christian gospel also includes the message that even in a brutal world life can be lived on a high plane. In Christian preaching the pendulum is likely to swing between an almost exclusive emphasis upon moral exhortation (as though it were the sole function of the pulpit to tell people to be good) and an almost exclusive emphasis upon forgiveness (as though the struggle for goodness were a lost cause and sinful man had no recourse except to trust that God will make right what man has made wrong). But neither emphasis is adequate without the other. Moral exhortation

[9] *Confessions*, X:7.

may become immoral if it forgets that no matter what heights of character a man may reach, he will still fall far short of his high calling in Christ Jesus. Moral exhortation may be stultifying if it blinds its hearers to the fact that they are caught in a social fabric which is the embodiment of injustices and cruelties for which every man must bear his share of the responsibility. But the assurance of forgiveness may be a deadening message if it implies that men may be content with evil because it is forgiven by the mercy of God, or if it encourages men to cease struggling against evil on the ground that it never can be overcome, or if it discourages men by teaching that the grace of God is confined to the exercise of mercy in another world but is never manifested as power to achieve better things in this world. The Christian gospel at its best has always been a moral incentive, not a sedative. It has always been assurance to every man that Power is with him in his moral night, a Power able to do exceeding abundantly above all that he can ask or think. It has always been a confidence that man is still an unprofitable servant, even when he has given his best, and that the grace of God does, in ways past man's conceiving, cover his mistakes and redeem him from his sin. The Christian gospel must be preached both as heroic demand and as the promise of mercy if it is to be true to its historic emphases or to the needs of the present time.

The preacher must make it unequivocally plain to every man that, from certain points of view, his Christian discipleship sometimes seems to involve a compromise with the Christian ideal. There are two sayings of Jesus which need to be studied with reference to each other. In the Sermon on the Mount, which abounds in startling commands cut-

ting directly across our commonly accepted ways of living,
he pointed out that what is wrong with most human life is
its major objective. "Seek ye first the kingdom of God and
His righteousness." At the end of the collection of sayings
which are traditionally known by that name comes the most
sweeping of all Jesus' ethical demands, "Be ye therefore perfect, as your Father in heaven is perfect." The perfect action
in any given situation is that which does most to promote the
kingdom of God. We sometimes wish that all life could be
catalogued in lists of Christian and unchristian actions, and
that all questions of conscience could be resolved by reference to the catalogue. But life is not so simple, and if it were,
the function of conscience would be at an end. Bishop F. R.
Barry has recently written that there are no Christian actions,
there are only Christian people acting.[10] Christian people
are people who are seeking first the kingdom of God. When-
ever we forget that, we become tangled in the confusions of
casuistry. The classic illustration is the account of a walk
down the Nevsky Prospect in the old St. Petersburg by
the American Minister to Russia, Andrew D. White, in
company with Leo Tolstoy. Tolstoy gave kopecks to every
beggar that asked for alms. Dr. White protested on the
ground that Tolstoy was encouraging a dependent pauperism
which was one of the critical social problems of the day.
Tolstoy replied that it was not his business to consider the
consequences of his action. The gospel said, "Give to him
that asketh thee" and it was his business only to obey the
gospel. But it is the business of every man to consider the
consequences of his actions. There are times when it is his
business to give, though it be his last crust of bread, and

[10] *Faith in Dark Ages*, pp. 41, 45.

there are times when it is his business to refuse to give, though his coffers may be full. The Christian must use his intelligence as well as his emotions in deciding such issues. His most painful decisions are those in which the active expression of good will toward one man or group involves the bringing of hardship upon other people. It is idle to argue that there are no situations in which one must choose the lesser of two evils. We all face such situations every day. They are involved in all discipline, in the allocation of our resources, in the protection of the weak, and often in the procedures of healing mind or body. In such conflicts of emotion, the difficulty must be resolved in the light of a larger good which takes into serious account the consequences of our action in the lives of other people. If such looking forward to the consequences of actions in determining their ethical validity is a compromise with the Christian ideal, then the preacher must not confuse those who trust his leadership by persuading them that such compromise can or should be avoided.

But the fact that ethical decisions are frequently complex rather than simple need never dull the moral edge of Christian preaching. It is still the task of the preacher to persuade men to seek first the kingdom of God and His righteousness, and to press toward the mark for the prize of the high calling of God in Christ Jesus. If the best that a man can do still leaves him an unprofitable servant, let him be sure that he is doing the best that he can, in the light of the best that he knows, in every concrete situation that confronts him. Let the preacher keep the layman in full view of all the issues, let him interpret to the layman the historic Christian tradition, let him respect the layman with whom

he differs as to the specific application of Christian principles
in moot questions, let him week in and week out challenge
the layman to measure up to the highest truth he sees, and
let him help the layman in the discovery of those resources
which make still higher achievements possible. Archbishop
Söderblom of Upsala once wrote that "the strength of our
Saviour was that he never became accustomed to the wrong."
His followers frequently do, and it is the task of the pulpit to
keep them from it. Perhaps there is no more urgent contemporary task for the preacher than to puncture the illusion
that because we humans cannot reach heaven at a single
bound, it makes no difference what kind of a hell we make for
ourselves and our kind. It is a sad day for the Christian
church when people can go out after hearing any sermon
which has not renewed their faith that even in a brutal and
sordid world life can be greatly lived.

V

The Christian gospel relates every man to the spiritual
energies that God has made available for the world through
Christ. It may not be the temper of our time to talk about
spiritual energies, but that capacity in every man which
makes him hunger for beauty and truth and goodness, and
which enables him to be satisfied from sources beyond himself, is something of which men are aware in every age. In
1928, when the wave of secularism was at its height in this
country, Dr. Henry S. Canby wrote in the *Saturday Review
of Literature* an editorial which he called a "Sermon on
Style," containing these words:

"We are scientific, utilitarian, practical. . . . But no one
of us is all scientific, utilitarian, practical. The waters still

run deep, even though the angel of the Old Testament seldom troubles them. A craving for beauty, a sense of awe, a
moral urge, the love of an ideal, the need of worship, the
belief in spiritual values, are of course as existent in a machine
age as in any other. . . . They must find expression somehow." [11]

No doubt there are countless people who have never recognized that they possess a capacity of this sort. They only
know that they are ill-adjusted to life and to themselves, that
life ought to hold something rich which they have missed,
and that they are subjected to strains for which they seem to
have no adequate resistance. They seem to be living in
closed rooms with no windows, to be like engines with no
motive power, to be like typewriters clicking out successions
of words that have no central meaning. They have imagined
that life could find an adequate purpose in the possession
of more and more things, but the more possessions they
have accumulated the more vividly they become conscious
of the aching of some unused capacity.

While President of the United States, Theodore Roosevelt wrote a significant letter to Frederic Mistral, the Pro-
vençal poet:

"All success to you and your associates! You are teaching
the lesson that none need more to learn than we of the West,
we of the eager, restless, wealth-seeking nation: the lesson
that after a certain not very high level of material well-being
has been reached, then the things that really count in life
are the things of the spirit. Factories and railroads are good
up to a certain point, but courage and endurance, love of
wife and child, love of home and country, love of lover for

[11] *Saturday Review of Literature*, December 22, 1928.

sweetheart, love of beauty in man's work and in nature, love and emulation of daring and of lofty endeavor, the homely work-a-day virtues and the heroic virtues—these are better still, and if they are lacking, no piled-up riches, no roaring, clanging industrialism, no feverish and many-sided activity shall avail either the individual or the nation. I do not undervalue these things of the nation's body: I only desire that they shall not make us forget that beside the nation's body there is also the nation's soul." [12]

It is the Christian faith that this capacity for a life of the spirit is the mark of man's kinship with the Creative Spirit of God, and that God is able to meet man's need for constant replenishment of the springs of his spiritual life. All the testimony of Christian history agrees in affirming the reality of this spiritual renewal which comes in response to faith, prayer, dedication, and outgoing service. Descriptions of the process by which that renewal comes are cast in a variety of word forms. William James spoke of "the higher energies that filter in" and J. A. Hadfield has written helpfully about the release of powers that are latent in the subconscious.[13] Henry N. Wieman has emphasized the part which autosuggestion plays in enabling the worshipper to make and keep contact with God.[14] To some people all such attempts to describe in psychological terms the basic religious experiences are obnoxious. It is not hard to understand the mood of the man in Sigrid Undset's Burning Bush who said: "I can take it into my head to believe it to be simply autosuggestion, when

[12] Scribner's Magazine (unidentified).
[13] James, Varieties of Religious Experience (Longmans, 1916 edition), p. 519; Hadfield, Psychology and Morals, chaps. 9-10.
[14] Methods of Private Religious Living, p. 35.

I feel that I am placed in connection with something and receive something as often as I pray to God. But nobody will get me to believe that autosuggestion can make people what the saints have been." [15] But analysis and definition of the process by which this renewal of life on the deeper levels comes about does not alter the essential fact that it takes place. Nor does it change the basic Christian contention that there are moral prerequisites to spiritual life at its freest and fullest. Nor does it invalidate the Christian faith that the Source of this spiritual life is the Spirit of God. He is not an abstraction but a Reality embracing in Himself all the powers and none of the limitations of what we vaguely call personality. In this enhancement of personal power and range of life, we touch Him and have dealings with Him.

It is hard to improve on Dr. L. P. Jacks's statement of this fact:

"There is that in the world, call it what you will, which responds to the confidence of those who trust it, declaring itself to them as a fellow-worker in the pursuit of the eternal values, meeting their loyalty to it with reciprocal loyalty to them, and coming in at critical moments when the need of its sympathy is greatest; the conclusion being, that wherever there is a soul in darkness, obstruction or misery, there also is a Power which can help, deliver, illuminate and gladden that soul. This is the helper of men . . . nearest at hand when the worst has to be encountered: the companion of the brave, the upholder of the loyal, the friend of the lover, the healer of the broken, the joy of the victorious—the God who is spirit, the God who is love." [16] One would question

[15] *Burning Bush*, p. 71.
[16] *Religious Perplexities*, p. 60.

the use of the impersonal rather than the personal pronoun. It is hard to see how "it" can be "the companion of the brave" and "the friend of the lover." A companion and a friend have the qualities which are expressed in companion-ship and friendship. He may be super-personal, but hardly sub-personal. The Christian tradition has affirmed its faith in a God who has personal relations with men when it has always used personal pronouns in its references to God. That relationship is in the realm which Dr. Jacks has described.

John Addington Symonds wrote of Michael Angelo: "Brooding over the sermons of Savonarola, the text of the Bible, the discourses of Plato, and the poems of Dante, he made his spirit strong in solitude by the companionship with everlasting thoughts." [17] Is that a lost art today? Certainly most of the ills of our tragic era can be traced back to the fact that men and women have lost contact with the realities that make the spirit strong. The preaching of the Word of God must lead wayfaring people to those springs. But first it must make men aware of the truth of the gospel which proclaims a God who can meet the need which every man knows, when the civilization in which man is enmeshed "leaves a dusty taste in his mouth," [18] a God Who can Him-self meet that man on the level of his capacity for spiritual life, and make that man a new creature in Christ

VI

The Christian gospel for every man is also an assurance that his sorrow can be used for spiritual ends. There may have been a time when the Christian pulpit dwelt too ex-

---

[17] *Renaissance in Italy, The Fine Arts*, p. 251.
[18] Walter Lippmann, *Preface to Morals*, p. 4.

clusively on the uses of adversity. Certainly some of the
older hymn books would seem to indicate that a dominant
note in the Christian church at one time was the proffer of
hope to sojourners in a vale of tears. Then came a change
of mood, and an insistence, also recorded in our hymn books,
that God is known not only in life's sterner experiences, but
also in happy, joyous hours.

> "O God, not only in distress,
> In pain and want and weariness,
> Thy tender Spirit stoops to bless,
> Thy will is done.
>
> In all that nature hath supplied,
> In flowers along the country side,
> In morning light, in eventide,
> Thy will is done.
>
> In youthful days, when joys increase,
> In light, in hope, in happiness,
> In quiet times of trustful peace,
> Thy will is done." [19]

That was a healthy note. Sometimes, however, the reaction
went so far that sorrow was almost ignored, the Christian
life was pictured as the gay adventuring of good companions
beneath sunlit skies, and church services were advertised as
"Pleasant Sunday Evening Hours," or as combinations of
interesting sermons, bright hymns, and happy fellowship.
All that is now in the past. It does not seem like an exaggeration, or as sentimentality, to speak of the world today as
a vale of tears. If the tears do not flow, it is because they are
held in check by thoughts too deep for tears. Sorrow is a

[19] From the hymn by Frederick Smith.

universal fact, but a universal fact which is particularized in the sorrows of individual men and women. The preaching of the Christian gospel is wide of the mark if it does not bring to every man the assurance that the bitterest disappointment can be used in the Providence of God for spiritual ends.

It is not for the preacher to set himself up as one who can find some easy explanation for every sorrow. He must point out that for much suffering we ourselves are directly responsible. The basic law, "Whatsoever a man soweth, that shall he also reap," must not be allowed to sink below the horizon. It must, however, always be interpreted in the light of the New Testament's frank recognition of the fact that very often a man is himself unaware of the tragic nature of his reaping. Is there a more ghastly picture of human life anywhere than the Spirit's verdict on the Laodiceans: "Thou sayest, I am rich, and increased with goods, and have need of nothing; and knowest not that thou art wretched, and miserable, and poor, and blind, and naked." [20] Sometimes the deepest tragedy is revealed where there is sin but no suffering, just as the bitterness of death is known not by those who grieve over the departure of one they have loved, but by those who cannot grieve because they did not love. "Why do you weep? Surely you did not love her?" asks the boy in the current novel about Maine life, and the old woman who has given the deceased loyal but loveless service for many years replies, "I weep because there is no grief." [21] "God does not always punish a nation by sending it adversity," wrote Dean W. R. Inge. "More often He gives the op-

[20] Revelation 3:17.
[21] Mary Ellen Chase, Windswept, p. 132.

pressors their hearts' desire, and sends leanness withal into their soul." [22] The dead conscience, the dead heart, the dead soul, these things, as well as the sharp stab of pain, must be included in our reckoning when we say that a man reaps what he sows. For these things as well as for suffering we must often bring ourselves to account.

The preacher must, if he can, without fruitless controversy, lead people beyond some of the popular but inadequate explanations of suffering. Among those who pride themselves that they are righteous, he will still find the belief that the sufferings of other people can confidently be attributed to the desire of God to punish those people for their sins. Jesus long ago pointed out that this was an unwarranted assumption when applied to the sufferings of people in Siloam, but his warning has not yet sunk into the consciousness of many people. However searching we may be in emphasizing the moral factor as a cause of our own disasters, we need to leave room for many other factors, known and unknown to us, when our brethren are in distress. In every American community there is an astonishing belief in primitive magic, as otherwise intelligent people seek to avert from themselves the incidence of hardship. Brides are sometimes more concerned that the hands of the clock shall be in what superstition calls the proper position at the hour of a wedding than they are about the cultivation of the spiritual attitudes which make for harmonious homes. A surprising number of superstitions linger on and claim not merely the amused and mocking observance of those who think that they might as well be on the safe side, since it does no harm to follow

[22] W. R. Inge, *Personal Religion and the Life of Devotion*, p. 58.

them, but also claim the serious trust of people who dilute their Christian faith with a large measure of belief in magic. There is also a widespread spirit of fatalism in the average American city or town. Along with the most conscientious consumption of vitamins in enormous quantities, with the most enthusiastic cooperation in programs for public health, with painstaking air raid precautions, and with genuine loyalty to the church and its faith is found a mixture of fatalistic determinism which finds expression in such popular sayings as, "if the germ is going to get you, it will get you," "if the bomb has your name on it, there is nothing you can do," "you won't die until your number is up." How much practical harm such superstitions and fatalisms do is problematical. The effect which they have in keeping people from entering fully into a Christian attitude toward suffering is considerable.

Let it be said again that the task and privilege of the preacher is not the explanation of suffering. Very often what he can do is to help people meet suffering which he can understand no more than they. Baron von Hugel tried to make this plain in a letter to a suffering and bewildered friend:

"How wonderful it is, is it not, that literally only Christianity has taught us the true peace and function of suffering! The Stoics tried the hopeless little game of denying its objective reality, or of declaring it a good in itself (which it never is), and the Pessimists attempted to revel in it, as a food for their melancholy, or as something to be avoided or explained. But Christ came, and He did not really explain it: He did far more, He met it, willed it, transformed it, and

He taught us how to do all this, or rather He himself does it within us, if we do not hinder the all-healing hands." [23]

One difficulty with the perennial human attempt to find an explanation for sorrow is that one might be able to explain every particular sorrow in the world, and still be unable to explain the fact of sorrow itself. Another difficulty is that sorrow which has been explained but which still must be met is still sorrow with all its bitterness, while sorrow which one has learned to meet and to transmute into sympathy and courage and faith has lost its bitterness, even though the atmosphere of mystery still surrounds the experience.

A beginning has been made when we accept the fact of suffering. That does not mean that we become inert before the prospect of preventible suffering threatening other people or ourselves. Nor does it mean that we ever cease to explore with every power at our command the mystery of suffering, or that we ever relax our efforts to prevent, alleviate, comfort, and heal. But when we have done all that, each of us must come to terms with the inexorable fact that in some sense suffering is a part of life. To rebel against that fact is misery. To submit to it is defeat. To accept it, and find ways of making it creative, is wisdom and the peace which is deeper than pain. J. Middleton Murry wrote in his introduction to the *Journal of Katherine Mansfield*:

"She suffered greatly; she delighted greatly. . . . She was utterly generous, utterly courageous; when she gave herself to life, to love, to some spirit of truth which she served, she gave royally. She loved life—with all its beauty and its pain;

[23] Friedrich von Hugel: *Selected Letters*, edited by Bernard Holland, p. 228.

she accepted life completely, and she had the right to accept it, for she had endured in herself all the suffering which life can lavish upon a single soul." [24] No doubt men will always hold varying opinions as to the direct interplay between the will of God and specific sorrows, but God would be disassociated from a large part of our life if He bore no responsibility for the fact that sorrow is an integral part of human experience. It is for the ministry of preaching to help people to accept that basic fact.

The preacher can also interpret suffering as an experience which can be used for creative purposes since God obviously so uses it. "All the good I ever got came to me in the shape of sorrow," wrote Thomas Carlyle. "There is nothing noble or godlike in this world but has in it something of infinite sadness." [25] Few people would make so sweeping a statement, but there are few who have not in some measure learned from the things which they have suffered. "I often feel," said George Tyrrell, "that if there were no temptations of mental darkness to wrestle with, I should not love the light as I do, and my spiritual lamp would go out." [26] Would any of us have learned to love the light if there had never been shadows? Who would value knowledge that had never known the agony of the mind which is the search for truth? When do we learn the deeper meanings of friendship, in the sharing of life's lighter moments, or in the sharing of peril, toil, and pain? When does suffering teach us most, when we resent its intrusion into our happiness most hotly, or

[24] P. 16.
[25] J. A. Froude, *Thomas Carlyle*, Vol. II, Chap. 2, p. 11.
[26] M. D. Petre, *Autobiography and Life of George Tyrrell*, Vol. II, p. 143.

when we resolve that, unwelcome visitor as it always is, we are going to bend it to creative uses?

If the preacher is to help people so to use sorrow, it will be by helping them to weave the strands of memory and thought and purpose that bind their experiences to the Cross of Christ. We are being told today with renewed insistence that the Cross is the channel through which God's forgiveness flows to man, but that man cannot find in the Cross a light that he can follow. Before the first half of this contention we must bow in humble reverence. It passes the bounds of human comprehension, but its truth is deep and central. But is it true that we do not find guidance as well as grace in the Cross? "Love so amazing, so divine, demands my heart, my life, my all." Always the revelation of God carries with it an obligation for men. Always the goodness of man is a response to the initiative of God. Always the perfection of God is a call to man to come up higher. It cannot be otherwise with the Cross. Calvary is a window into heaven—let us gratefully acknowledge what it teaches us of the forgiving love of a Father Who is forever giving Himself to redeem His world. But Calvary is also a challenge and a promise to every man. Here was human tragedy at its blackest, judged by the wisdom of the world. Earth's noblest life cut off just as its usefulness was beginning, so it would seem. But things are seldom what they seem. The ministry of Jesus was not ended. It was just beginning. The Cross marks the most creative act in history. Who could measure the faith and life and victory that are traceable back to its influence as their origin? You and I are not Christ, and we are not to tell people that they are the Saviours of the world. He occupies a place that is unique. But we are to persuade men and women engulfed beneath the tide of sorrow that has swept over the world that this Cross does show men and women like us how we are to try to meet the grim side of human experience. Standing face to face with this Cross, we are, as the ambassadors of Christ to say, "Have faith in God, Who in a Providence the mystery of which our minds do not penetrate, uses even the crosses of the world for the world's healing!" Wasted suffering is the most terrible kind of waste. If the Christian gospel does not even attempt to answer the "Why?" which is wrung from the lips of every sufferer, it does assure us that no suffering need be wasted, for God uses it for creative purposes when it is met in the spirit of the Cross of Christ.

Without attempting even to name the varied ways in which sorrow and suffering are used for the enrichment of life (every pastor can read them in letters of gold if he will glance over his parish list with an imaginative eye), we must not pass by in silence one use to which sorrow can be put which the very times we live in underscore today. Sorrow can be made one of the links binding together a broken world in sympathy and mutual faith. The sorrows which follow in the wake of war can become the common experience out of which all peoples derive the determination to end war. But, beyond that, every mysterious, undeserved, irrational pain of body or spirit is part of the load which someone must bear as the price of mankind's ignorance, mankind's folly, mankind's sin. It is not only that such suffering spurs on the relentless search of science for the cause and cure of obscure disease, and that the woes of innocent people sting the consciences of men with social vision, strengthening their resolve never to give up the struggle

until this or that wrong is righted. Suffering does bring about
such joining of hands in fellow-feeling and in effort to com-
bat wrongs. But often the sufferers themselves are out of
these battles. The victim of a disease for which science has
as yet found no cure can seldom do much about that problem as it affects other people. But even for him, his suffering
is a link with humanity. It is his share of the total human
load of ignorance, as the sufferings of the persecuted are part
of the frightful human cost of hate. Even the indignities of
loathsome disease and the agonies caused by human cruelty
take on dignity when their victims are aware of being bound
in a bundle of life with the ignorant and the malignant
through their pain. Jesus' prayer on the Cross for his tor-
turers is the expression of this spiritual unity in so pure a
form that we give over all attempts at analysis, and humbly
thank God for the faith behind it.

The little bulletin of the Class in Personal Religion of the
Cathedral Church of St. Paul in Boston once published a
brief tale based upon a dream which crossed the mind of a
sufferer from a disease for which there was little hope of
escape. He saw a mighty army of people moving across a
plain, bearing burdens labelled "Injustice," "Bad Inherit-
ance," "Vicarious Sufferings," "Grief," "Disease." He
thought of his own broken hopes, thwarted ambitions, en-
forced idleness and weakness, blank prospects. Through his
rebellious thoughts there came a voice, saying: "You sought
to be a leader of the host; you chose to be a maker of the
road . . . It could not be . . . You are a burden bearer of
mankind. There is the burden of the race, the burden of its
folly and its wrong, its ignorance, its stupid prejudice, its
sin, its wilful violation of law, its innocent transgression of

the rule. Someone must carry that." Then the writer, Alexis Stein, addresses his readers directly:

"Oh, fellow-bearers of the load we did not choose, the load we fain would have some other carry if we could, remember this—the burden bearers help the world along. I know not how it is. I know not all the law. I am only sure of this—the fight that each man fights behind his chamber door for courage and for patience and for faith, he fights not for himself alone, he fights for all mankind; he fights as one who is a helper of his kind, as a blood brother of that One, who in little Galilee, obscure, almost alone, was wounded for our transgressions and bruised for our iniquities, and who upon the cross became the Burden Bearer of the human race." [27]

"Doth God exact day-labour, light denied?" There are times when "They also serve, who only stand and wait," [28] if their waiting is a deepening of their fellowship with humanity. No preaching of the gospel to a world in which suffering is writ large can proclaim the whole truth if it does not make it plain to folk in the dazed bewilderment of sorrow that God can and does so use faith-ful grief.

VII

The Christian gospel, therefore, comes to men caught in the frustrations of ordinary life and in the cataclysmic tragedies of extraordinary times, demanding their faith, their loyalty, their love, and promising them the power of spirit necessary for growth and achievement, a new quality of life, and a sense of being befriended by the Eternal Friend of

[27] Issue of February 24, 1928.
[28] John Milton, *On His Blindness*.

mankind. It comes to all men and it comes to every man.
All its challenges and promises become personal in the Man
of Nazareth. The response which makes it real must also
be personal in the mind and will of every man. "A man will
not roll in the snow for a stream of tendency by which all
things fulfill the law of their being," wrote G. K. Chesterton in his interpretation of St. Francis. "He will not go
without food in the name of something not ourselves, which
makes for righteousness. He will do these things when he
is in love. Francis was a lover of God and he was really and
truly a lover of men . . . As he did not love humanity but
men, so he did not love Christianity, but Christ." [29] It is
the aim of the preacher so to unveil the splendor of Christ
to every man as to elicit such loyal response.

In the long run, every man follows the flag of his faith. He
becomes, to some extent, what he puts his deepest trust in.
"The just shall live by his faith." But the unjust also lives by
his faith. He is unjust because his innermost conviction is
that the universe is founded on lies, not truth. Men do not
lift themselves by their own boot-straps to higher levels;
they are lifted by dynamic realities in which they have faith.
Let the preacher be sure that he does not obscure the reality
of faith in Christ behind theological subtleties and tech-
nicalities. It is such faith that moulds character. At the
dedication of a building in memory of Harlan P. Amen, one
time Head Master of the Phillips Exeter Academy, one who
had been closely associated with him, Mr. George B. Rogers,
said:

"Others might calculate their own advantage but he saw
no advantage but the school's . . . The Greek ideal was

[29] *St. Francis of Assisi*, p. 21.

'nothing in excess.' His spirit was of a different lineage, the Christian—the spirit of the devotee, whose life is one magnificent excess, unreasonable and ruinous, flung into the face of fate on the Christian chance that sacrifice and service of one's kind is somehow at the basis of our moral universe."

Without such devotion to the point of dedication life is cramped. Life lived by such devoted faith turns "the Christian chance" into the Christian assurance. It becomes an assurance that Christ is not only the Way, but also the Truth concerning the Life that reaches beyond the limits of anything that this passing world can bound. It is the function of the preacher so to create faith in his hearers, that each man will forget the preacher, and finding himself face to face with One who constrains us to call him Lord, will say directly to him, "Lord, to whom shall we go? Thou hast the words of Eternal life!"

V

THE WORD AND THE PASTOR

"And he continued there . . . teaching the Word of God among them."

ACTS 18:11.

THE WORD AND THE PASTOR

D R. JOHN OMAN said in one of his talks "Concerning the Ministry," that "the old name 'the Ministry of the Word' includes not only your preaching but all your work, if you understand by the Word of God what even the Scriptures only serve." [1] Much of a minister's preaching is done outside the pulpit. He ought not to become self-conscious about this. Many of the professional mannerisms which develop in ministers, making them the easy prey of the caricaturist, grow out of the minister's awareness that wherever he is and whatever he is doing, he is preaching. The common prayer for all sorts and conditions of ministers is they will forget that they are preachers and be content to be men! But nothing can alter the fact that the minister is always preaching something. If he becomes a pompous ecclesiastic or a theatrical egotist or a dry-as-dust pedant, by his very presence he proclaims the emptiness of what Baron von Hugel called "churchiness," the pathos of using the church as a ladder for personal pride, and the sin of supposing that a display of learning is the cure of souls. An earlier generation more frequently than ours spoke of the minister as a "man of God." If anything can save the minister both from the shallow professionalism which magnifies the external eccentricities of his calling, and from the shallow secularism which blots out all distinctions between his high calling and others, it is the aspiration to be what

[1] *Concerning The Ministry*, p. 165.

every true minister knows he never can worthily be, a man of God. Only God-consciousness can save a man from self-consciousness. If a minister must in all his work preach something, let him pray that in all his life and work he may preach the Word of God.

There is a fine word for this side of the minister's work, coming down to us from New Testament times, and even from Jeremiah. The Lutherans use it habitually when they address a minister as "pastor." It is not so popular perhaps today as once it was, and this shift in mood may constitute one of the church's major problems. A young theological graduate from Oxford remarked to an American friend that he did not believe that British congregations were anxious to be shepherded as American church people were. The American replied that the Oxonian had misinterpreted the temper of American churchmen if he imagined that many of them thought themselves to be hungry sheep looking up to be fed. It may be that this shift in mood is due to a change in our idea of what a shepherd is. In modern times we think of a shepherd as one who drives his sheep. In gospel times the shepherd was the leader of his flock, going before them up whatever steep ascents, and into whatever thickets or dangers lay in the way. It may be that a revival of the New Testament position of a shepherd would give new life to the pastoral aspect of the ministry.

As a matter of fact no minister can drive a modern congregation. In most free churches ecclesiastical authority is no greater than the capacity for leadership of the pastor and those with whom he shares responsibility for the church's usefulness. This is as true in those churches which by their constitutions vest legal authority in the ministry and elected officers as in those where no such powers are granted. Legally constituted authority can be effective over church property, but never nowadays over church members. The only authority which commands their allegiance is a spiritual authority which they recognize as authentic. Little men with an exaggerated idea of their own importance are no more influential when clothed with ecclesiastical status than they are in other spheres of life. A pastor who so misconceives his function as to suppose that it is his duty to issue orders, give commands, and lay down directions for which he expects obedience by reason of his office has sadly mistaken the results of the Protestant Reformation and the temper of the American people. It is well for the Christian church that this is so. The church is too vital to respond to would-be dictators or to be driven pell-mell in any direction at a word of command. Any pastor, however, who has even modest gifts for leadership, who has in some measure the character which wins confidence, and has a religion which is transparently honest and genuine will have more authority than he wants. He will be terrified at times by the trusts that are imposed in him. He will hesitate even to make suggestions because his tentative and halting thoughts are too often received by others with a confidence which he himself does not place in them. He will never bewail the fact that excommunication has ceased to have terrors, because his supreme concern is not with shutting men out but rather with drawing them in to the fellowship of Christ. He will never waste energy regretting the lost authority of the ministry, for he will be constantly amazed at the readiness of all kinds of people to follow a pastor who has no desire to drive, but who is willing to do his poor best to lead the way.

II

Being a pastor is, of course, being a friend. That is one of
the greatest privileges of the ministry, one of its fine arts, and
one of its dangers. It is only from the financial point of view
(and then it is far from being universally true) that the ministry is an underpaid calling. Among other rewards which
escape all known methods of calculation is a wealth of friendship which pours in upon him in a measure far beyond anything that he can personally deserve. No one will ever be
able to do justice to what this tide of friendliness means to
the minister who is its surprised and somewhat puzzled and
deeply grateful recipient. In most walks of life friendships
are made rather cautiously, they develop slowly, they are
hedged about by reservations and guarded commitments,
they generally keep open some ways of escape in case retreat
looks more alluring than standing one's ground. But unless
a minister presumes upon the privileges of his office, or proves
himself unworthy of friendship, he is included in the circles
of friendship with a readiness which humbles him. For most
people friendships unfortunately are circumscribed by arti-
ficial barriers. People make friends with other people who
live in the same neighborhood, or have similar income, or
are in the same business, or have the same hobby, or went
to the same college, or have children in the same school.
They have acquaintances in other groups, but they have
subtle and not so subtle ways of limiting friendship to those
like themselves. A minister belongs to no clique, his life is
enriched with the friendship of a wide variety of people, and
he would be put to it to say from whom he receives most,
those who are conspicuous in the eyes of the community or

those generally regarded as underprivileged. He at least is among the highly privileged in the wealth of friendliness in the midst of which his life is set.

There is nothing more to be said about the art of friendship, for ministers or others, since Emerson wrote that "the only way to have a friend is to be one." But there are peculiar perils lurking for the minister in this matter of being a friend. One peril is that in being a friend he may cease to be the minister, or that in being the minister he may never really become a friend. A New England village church was about to hold a meeting to decide which of two young men it would call to be its minister. The doctor of the village, a sincere man with a wisdom gathered through years of intimate knowledge of that town, finding himself unexpectedly unable to attend the meeting, sent his vote in these words: "I am for the man that everybody does not call by his first name." The common American practice of calling the minister by his given name is not necessarily bad. But that doctor did not want as a minister a man who would be simply a good fellow, everybody's pal, with nothing distinctive about the quality of the friendship he had to give. The doctor was shrewd enough to have at his tongue's end a rough and ready formula for guarding against that possibility—a formula which might, of course, have excluded the very man he wanted. Perhaps, with equal wisdom, he might have said: "I am not for the man that no one would ever dream of calling by his first name." For the minister who is so conscious of himself as a minister that he cannot become a friend is as ineffective as the genial soul whom everybody likes but whom no one ever thinks of as the representative of the church of Jesus Christ. T. R. Glover has recorded a

caustic comment on the head of a college, of whom it was
said: "If he would leave off caring for his students' *souls*,
and care for *them*, he would do better." [2] Of course the truth
is that the students' souls are not separable from the students,
and the college head cannot care now for one and then for
the other. But he must not care for the students and forget
that they have souls, nor care for their souls and forget that
they are his friends. So a friendly minister cares about people just as people, and he also cares about that capacity for
infinitely richer life with which God has endowed every
man, which for want of any adequate term we sometimes
speak of as the soul. It does not make much difference what
the people call their minister (so long as they do not call
him "Reverend Jones") if they really feel that he is their
friend, and at the same time never forget that he is their
minister, ordained to the service of the church of Jesus
Christ.

One of the subtle dangers that besets the minister is that
of restricting the bounds of his friendship within limits that
are narrower than the limits of his congregation. The man
who complained that, although his minister had been very
kind to him, he never quite knew whether he was regarded as
a friend or as "just one of the parish," had a legitimate complaint. He wanted to be a person, not merely a member of
the church. He wanted to be sure that any friendship shown
him was genuine, not merely the performance of a professional obligation. But he implied a belief that the minister
put his congregation into two categories, those whom he
wanted as friends and those to whom he had to be friendly.
Any such classification of people is contrary to the genius of

[2] *The Jesus of History*, p. 136.

the pastorate. A pastor is a human being, and there are some people with whom he will have more common interests and tastes than with others. If he has a congregation of many members, it will be a constant sorrow to him that he cannot demonstrate his friendship to them all in practical ways as he would like to do. Inevitably, circumstances and duties will throw him into the company of some members of his congregation more than others. All that is to be taken for granted. But he must not become a member of a clique. He must not identify himself with some particular social group. He must not let any group annex him, or make him a vested interest, on whom they have a proprietary claim. (Principal James Denney, of Glasgow, once said to a group of theological students, "Don't become the pet lamb of your flock; be their shepherd.") [3] Above all the pastor must not in his own mind recognize differences between people in his congregation insofar as his relationship with them is concerned. He is the pastor of all. That means that he is the friend of them all. If he does not have the gift for friendship with all kinds of people, if he has to force himself to try to be friendly as an unwelcome duty to which he submits as part of the price he pays for the privilege of electrifying the world on Sunday mornings, he had better not be a minister at all. For a minister is a pastor and a pastor is a friend.

III

A pastor is also a counsellor. That does not mean that it is his prerogative or duty to give people the answers to all their questions or to tell them what to do in all their perplexities.

[3] *Letters of Principal James Denney,* edited by James Moffatt, p. viii.

Nothing could be more presumptuous than such a rôle for any man, and few things could be worse for the people of a church than to have omniscience on tap in the minister's study, even if that were possible, as in the Providence of God it is not. There are three contributions which a minister can make to people who want counsel. He can make available to them whatever range of experience he may have had, which has probably touched life at more crucial points and in a wider variety of circumstance than is possible for most people. (In so doing he must zealously guard the confidences which are his because of his pastoral office, refusing to retail even anonymously the experience of one person to another. But whatever knowledge about life these experiences have opened up for him is his to share where it is needed and desired.) But he can do more than this. He can be an accessible, trusted, impersonal person who through discussion can help individuals to understand their own problems better and to find their own solutions for them. But the best thing he can do goes beyond this. He can help people to find their religious resources in God who can give them the help that they most need. God seldom speaks through ministers in oracular tones the final word on the problems either of individuals or society. But some of us have known ministers through whom God spoke to us the words that helped us find our own way through some parts of the wilderness.

It is frequently said nowadays that the minister should keep office hours like the physician, and that the people should be encouraged to go to him with their spiritual problems as they go to other specialists with other problems. Certainly every minister should be available for people who want to talk over their difficulties and their plans with him, and they should know that they are welcome. Whether he follows a schedule of office hours, or can be seen by appointment, or has some other plan for devoting a measure of his time to personal interviews, the people should be clearly informed what that plan is, so that they will not feel, when they come to see him, that they are intruding upon the time which he must set aside for his other work.

He must remember that he is a minister, not a psychiatrist or a social worker. He ought to know enough about mental hygiene to be familiar with the more common mental illnesses, some of which are very common after a dozen years of financial depression and world conflict. He ought to know enough about social work to know what the resources of his community are for people who have problems, and how to relate people in need with the provisions which the community has made for just such situations. He must divest himself of the erroneous idea that he is a good man talking with sinful people, or a man who lives on one spiritual plane talking down to people on another. He must be willing to listen far more than he talks. He must never be shocked, however much people try to shock him, and he must eschew the cheap device of trying to demonstrate his humanity by shocking them. He must not argue with people, for that simply backs them up against the wall where they are concerned with defending themselves, not with solving their problems.

He must not expect people to go from the interview with what they came for all wrapped up and delivered in neat packages of advice. He must be content if, in the course of the interview, they have seen more clearly the alternative courses open to them, have understood better where those courses will lead and what they will cost, have seen their problems more sharply against truer perspectives, have appreciated more fully their own capacities and their resources in God, and have gained courage and decisiveness for the making of their own decisions. The minister's temptation is to dominate the minds of other people, to tell them what to do, and to make their decisions for them. Very often this is what people want, and they will be most grateful when the minister relieves them of the obligations of hard thought and conscientious choice. But very often the most useful interview is one for which some one is not so grateful, because he goes away still confronted with the necessity for making his own decision, which he has wanted to avoid. It is a bad sign when too many people in a congregation think exactly as their minister does on all subjects. It was said of Dr. Jowett of Balliol College, Oxford, "that he sent out more pupils who were widely unlike himself than any Oxford teacher of his time." Dr. George Herbert Palmer once wrote, "Every teacher knows how easy it is to send out cheap editions of himself, and in his weaker moments he inclines to issue them. But it is ignoble business." [4] It is no more noble when it is done by a pastor.

If the minister is the kind of man who by his very presence communicates vitality and confidence to other people, the people who consult him are fortunate. An Oxford student who had visited Canon Barnett in his study at Toynbee Hall wrote years afterward: "I remember so well the mixture of enthusiasm and clearheadedness with which one left his study at Toynbee. I felt . . . that the whole world

[4] *Ethical Instruction in Schools*, p. 45.

ought to be conquered and could be conquered." [5] Such influence, however, is a gift of God, and a minister had better leave the disposition of it to the Creator. He can try to be an intelligent, informed, understanding, sincere consultant. If he has the gift of dynamic influence, he will probably not know it. Like the Bluebird, it will never be his if he seeks it.

But, however valuable and fruitful this type of office consultation may be, it can never take the place of the more casual contacts between pastor and people which have been traditional in the Christian ministry. Those contacts, which are made through regular visitation of the homes of the people and through such other methods as a minister may devise for this age when it is increasingly difficult to find people in their homes, are the indispensable background for everything the minister does. They are the richest reward of the ministry, and constitute the field in which unpremeditated opportunities for usefulness most frequently appear. The number of people who will take the initiative in seeking interviews with a minister will depend on several factors: the degree to which his preaching makes people feel that they want to consult with him; the assurance people have that their confidence will be respected and that the minister will not use them in his sermons even as anonymous illustrations; the physical arrangements of his place for interviews and the ease with which he can be seen without having the interview either a furtive meeting or a public meeting; above all, the confidence which people have in the minister's sin-

[5] H. O. Barnett, *Canon Barnett: His Life, Work and Friends*, p. 316.

cerity, his desire to be of help to them insofar as he can, and the reality of his own religious life. But however successful the minister may be in meeting these conditions, there will be some people who need his help who will never come to him unless the way has been paved by the establishment of a friendship on a more personal basis, just as there are some people who will never come to a Protestant minister because at best an interview with a Protestant minister lacks the impersonality of the Roman Catholic confessional. And there are some people who will never come at all under any circumstances. The minister must keep his contacts with all these people. He must know them where they live, not exclusively under the roof of the church. He must know them not only when they are aware of problems weighing heavily upon them, but also when they are engaged in the normal round of life. If he is a discerning friend, he will sometimes discover needs, spiritual and otherwise, of which they are not aware, and it may be his good fortune to be able to help them solve problems which they did not know they had and which they did not know they had solved.

A pastor must have a sort of sixth sense for knowing when and where he can render such aid. It is a principle of counselling, as currently understood, that results are obtained only when the person with a problem is ready to work out his problem with a counsellor. A minister who forces his way into the privacy of individuals, invades the legitimate reticences of self-respecting people, or demands as his right the privilege of discussing personal matters which the people most concerned do not want to discuss, defeats the very purpose which he seeks to further. But a minister who neither demands nor presumes, but is himself ready to talk over personal problems which people want to bring out into the light with an understanding friend, will find people all the readier for his help if he has shown enough personal interest in them to come to them as their pastor.

An almost universal human need has been expressed in these lines by Jeanne D'Orge which appeared in a daily paper a few years ago under the title, "The Interpreter":

"I wish there were some one
 Who would hear confession.
 Not a priest—I do not want to be told of my sins;
 Not a mother—I do not want to give sorrow;
 Not a friend—she would not know enough;
 Not a lover—he would be too partial;
 Not God—He is far away;
 But some one who would be friend, lover, mother, priest,
   God, all in one,
 And a stranger besides—who would not condemn or interfere;
 Who, when everything is said from beginning to end,
 Would show the reason of it all
 And tell you to go ahead
 And work it out your own way." [6]

Perhaps something like that is what the pastor at his best can be, except that he is not a stranger but a friend in whose presence one can be sincere, and that his greatest service is to help his friends to have confidence that God is not far away but nearer than they have ever known, with spiritual resources available for them which are more than adequate for any difficulty with which life may confront them.

[6] *New York Times*, Book Section, July 7, 1940.

IV

The pastor is also an administrator. He may wish that this were not the case. If he enjoys preaching and friendly contacts with individuals, he may not find the detailed work of a church organization to his liking. If he is an administrator by nature, he may revel in that side of his work, to the neglect of his study and his visiting, but the common opinion of church trustees that ministers do not know much about practical matters would seem to indicate that good administrators are rare in the ministry. It has been suggested that our small churches ought to be consolidated into large regional churches capable of supporting a diversified ministry, so that men with administrative gifts can devote themselves entirely to the tasks of organization and other men confine themselves to other aspects of this calling in which so many varied gifts can be usefully employed. A few large churches in populous cities have been able to employ such variegated staffs of ministers, and beginnings along this line have been made in certain rural "larger parishes." There is a great deal to be said for the proposal, although there will probably always be many people who will find it harder to be at home in a large consolidated church than in the more intimate fellowship of a smaller group, and it must always be remembered that over-specialization may have the same narrowing influence upon the minister that it has upon men in some of the professions. However that may be, there is little likelihood that such a transformation of American church life will come about in the near future, and most pastors will continue to be like circus acrobats riding several horses at the same time.

If a minister happens to be the kind of man who finds administrative details a burden there is all the more reason for his being scrupulously faithful in his attention to them. There is no work worth doing which does not involve some elements of drudgery. Mr. Van Wyck Brooks has spoken for the writers: "No good writer has ever liked drudgery, nor has any good writer ever permitted any one else to do his drudgery for him." [7] The average member of the average congregation is not unacquainted with work which seems to him monotonous. Some of them feel that all of their working hours are filled with work which in itself has little or no interest for them. It may be part of the spiritual discipline necessary for the minister's own development that he have his share of work which he would not choose, but which is necessary to keep the church organization functioning. Certainly being an administrator will help him to understand people who work in offices rather than in studies. At any rate, his fidelity to this side of the pastorate, insofar as the responsibility for it is placed upon him, is an obligation which as a man of honor he owes to those who have trusted him with it.

V

The pastor also has the opportunity to be, if he will, a sort of liaison officer between his church and the community of which it is a part. If he feels that his church has no responsibility to the community this opportunity will not constitute any problem for him, although, if that is the case, he has another more serious problem of which he may be totally unaware—himself. The minister is not the only link between

[7] *New England Indian Summer*, p. 174.

his church and the community, of course. In most communities, a good share of the people who are doing the creative
and sustaining work for the public welfare are in the
churches. Each one of them is a sort of two-way street along
which traffic flows from the church to the community, and
from the community into the church. But the minister
stands in a peculiar place. It depends in very considerable
measure upon him how much sense of responsibility for
community life exists in his church. He has it in his keeping
whether or not the services of worship of his church have an
intelligent concern for the community in the prayers that
are offered and in the resolves that are made before God.
He is the one person who can do most to keep his church
sensitive to opportunities for cooperation with other organizations working for the betterment of the community. That
is his great privilege, and it is one of his most perplexing
problems. For the community is an octopus. Its tentacles
are numerous and tenacious. No man is in the ministry very
long without seeing some of his colleagues go under, dragged
down in the clutches of innumerable community interests
which have seized them and made it impossible for them to
keep afloat intellectually, spiritually, or as servants of the
church. President Charles W. Eliot in 1921 wrote to a ministerial friend: "I notice in a good many young men that
their religion seems to consist chiefly in a burning desire to
be of service to those they live with and to their own community, but I cannot help thinking that 'to walk humbly with
thy God' is a very important part of religion." [8] No minister
in his zeal for community service can afford to forget that
central emphasis of his ministry. Few ministers can respond

[8] Henry James, *Life of Charles W. Eliot*, Vol. II, p. 298.

to all the demands which their communities would make upon their time and energy. A minister is not called upon to be the errand-boy or the salesman for agencies of community service, however worthy they may be. But any minister loses something vital out of his life and message if he has no points of contact with the organized work for social welfare that is being carried on in the community which he serves. It is a helpful means of continuing education for himself if he is generally working in an official capacity with at least one social agency outside his own church. If his church happens to be conspicuously lacking in a sense of community responsibility, it may be wise for him to take an even larger part in civic affairs, in order to weave more strands of sympathy and understanding between his church and some of the welfare work which had its origin in the church but is now wisely separate from it. If his church tends to neglect other sides of its manifold life in favor of community service, it may be wise for the minister to take very little part in such activities. Even so, there is no danger that the social agencies of a community will be too well understood even by the people of the churches, or that the contributions of religion to social work will be too well understood even by those busiest in serving the welfare of the community, and a pastor who cares about the life of his community is in a unique position to acquire the information necessary to interpret each group to the other.

Fortunately there are a number of trends today both in work for community welfare and in the church which make such interpretation timely and possible. Modern social workers are increasingly interested in case work. They are concerned about the individual, about the inner life which makes him what he is and makes him do what he does, and about the resources which he has within himself for solving his problems and changing his environment. They are interested in the causes of social ills, in the measures which can be taken to prevent them, and in the healing of damaged souls as well as in the alleviation of suffering. They are interested in a partnership of doctor, psychiatrist, social worker, and minister, so that in cases of sickness the whole man and not merely the disease may be treated and if possible cured. They are interested in organizing the whole community so that all its resources may be utilized in a cooperative effort to build a sound community life in which the individual may realize his highest possibilities, and in which the community may have the benefit of the fullest possible contribution from every individual. These are also the interests of the Christian church. It is unfortunate when social work animated by such purposes is regarded by church people as a secular rival for their time and effort. Church people who are serving such purposes are doing church work wherever they are, whether their activity is carried on in the name of the church and on its premises or elsewhere. It is equally unfortunate when people engaged in this kind of social work feel that the church is not interested in what they are doing, or fail to appreciate the religion which is inarticulate in the service which they render, or do not see that an articulate religious faith in the love of God would add depth and richness and power to all that they hope to do with and for their fellowmen. The pastor who is alive to the needs of his community, and appreciates the constructive forces that are at work in its life can be a helpful and sorely needed interpreter.

VI

The pastor is also a sort of liaison officer between the local church which he serves and the church at large. This is a function which he will almost certainly never be permitted to forget. Every day's mail will bring him reminders that his denominational headquarters and many other headquarters doing work in the name of the church have not forgotten him. At least he is on their mailing-lists. All the devices of an ingenious mechanical age are employed to make him forget that the communication he receives is also being received that morning by thousands of other ministers, and to persuade him that what the postman has brought to him is a personal message direct from the study of the famous Dr. Silvertongue to the struggling brother in New Jersey or Connecticut. The psychology of such promotional literature is not infallible, for what the struggling brother in New Jersey wants to be made to remember is the very fact which the pseudo-personal letter tries to conceal. He wants to be reminded that he is one of a great band of ministers who are doing their best to serve the kingdom of God and that the local church of which he has the honor to be minister is part of the universal fellowship of Christians. He does not want to think of himself as a promoter, and he does not intend to be a promoter. He does want to think of himself as called to be a link between a local fellowship of Christians and the wider fellowship of the Christian church. He is glad to be told that his church is an indispensable unit in the chain of Christian faith and love which girdles the globe. He is thankful that God can use his church, its prayers, its life, its gifts in the world-wide work of the church. He wants all the in-

formation, all the inspiration, all the suggestions which can
help his church to do its part. He knows that he is inclined
to go to sleep on his job, and that he needs to be prodded
and challenged, and he is grateful for such stimulation. He
finds it most stimulating when it comes as a simple, straightforward story of what the church at large is doing and what
he can do to help, and when it is freest from the slogans and
catchwords which seem so easily to become the shop-worn
stock-in-trade of the promoters of religion. He knows that
the people of his church are busy people, with many responsibilities and cares, and that some of them will not have a
very vivid sense of their wider Christian affiliation unless he
helps them to understand their privilege and its concurrent
responsibility. He is glad that he can be a liaison officer between a local church and the whole church.

For an increasing number of ministers a denominational
affiliation is anything but an unmixed blessing. In student
gatherings and young people's conferences the question is
frequently asked in cavalier fashion, "Why don't you get rid
of all these denominations and have just one Protestant
church?" The obvious answers need not be rehearsed here,
except to point out that some methods of getting rid of the
Protestant churches would get rid of the Protestant church
at the same time. By cancelling out all the digits in the
column, the result would be zero. The church is not a disembodied spirit, as perhaps we sometimes wish it were. It is
an organization, and all constructive efforts to unify the
organization of the church must go through the laborious
process of fitting together harmoniously the organizations
that now exist. That may be brought to pass some day with
unexpected suddenness, but if so it will be because that

denouement has been preceded by a long and faithful process of conferences, adjustments, cooperative undertakings, and prayers. The minister who cares about the unity of the Christian church will not spend his time berating the churches because they are not unified, but will find more useful employment for his energies in helping along some of the cooperative enterprises in his own community that are actually making for the unity of the Christian church. And he will be careful to see that, while thus engaged, he does not weaken any of the churches which now exist.

It is to be hoped that when the unity of the churches is achieved, it will be a unity of churches that come together in their strength, because they know that the faith which unites them is greater than the beliefs on which they differ, and because they know that only a united church can do what the church of God is called to do in helping to unite a world which has been broken to pieces. Two sick churches uniting do not necessarily make one healthy church. Each may simply aggravate the illness of the other, and the last state of both be worse than the first. The prime essential for Christian unity is that there should be churches strong in spirit and effective in organized activities to unite. Therefore the minister who is deeply concerned about the unity of the Christian church knows that there is no incompatibility between his loyalty to the whole church of Christ and his present loyalty to the denomination in which he now serves. He may suspect that the man who is careless about his denominational obligations would be careless about his obligations to any church, united or fractional. He will divest himself, of course, of any feeling that his denomination is superior to others. He will take the trouble to explore the history and to try to understand the present practice of other churches than his own. But by the same token he will try to appreciate his own church also, remembering, as Emerson once put it, that "every ship looks romantic but the one you are on." He will study the history of his own denomination, will understand what contributions it has made to the broad stream of Christian influence, will ask himself what are its distinctive features that ought to be conserved in a united church, and will carry his fair share of the detailed work which is necessary to make a denomination a cooperative fellowship of individual churches. He will know what his denomination is doing in the world, and what he can do to help. Dean Inge once asked, "He who loves not his home and country which he has seen, how shall he love humanity in general which he has not seen?" [9] If a minister cares nothing about the branch of the Christian church in which he has served, what likelihood is there that he will be a very useful addition to the united church which as an organization has not yet come into being? It is the minister's opportunity both to work for the church of his dreams, and to play his part in the actual church of the present. As the pastor of a congregation, he can be the leader along both lines of effort.

VII

Every pastor is a teacher. Not only does he inevitably teach something from the pulpit—even if it be only that the church is a dull place unrelated to life—but he also has a large measure of responsibility for what the church as a whole teaches. That the church has been inadequate in its teach-

[9] W. R. Inge, *Outspoken Essays*, p. 58.

ing function may be taken for granted, although it may be that the church's failure to produce Christian character in those who come under its educational influences has been exaggerated because of the inability of statistical methods accurately to appraise character. What can be accurately tested is the ignorance of the facts concerning the Christian tradition and the Christian teachings on the part of those who have grown up in the midst of a supposedly Christian culture. By every test that ignorance is appalling. Dr. J. H. Oldham reported in 1940 that the evidence collected by chaplains with the British Army suggested, "that ninety per cent of the youth of the nation have ceased to have any living connection with Christianity, and that there is nothing to keep them from becoming a prey to any pagan force that may arise." [10] President Mildred McAfee recently wrote concerning the American college students whom she has had opportunity to observe at close range: "Of Wellesley students 98.8 per cent enter college with some church affiliation. Approximately the same proportion are essentially ignorant of the religious tradition to which they claim allegiance." [11] Such statements, the accuracy of which few ministers would contest, obviously lay an urgent task at the door of the Christian church.

For the sake of perspective, it should be remembered that the divorce between youth and the church has always been a serious problem. Lyman Beecher wrote in his reminiscences of student days at Yale at the end of the eighteenth century: "College was in a most ungodly state; the college church was almost extinct. Most of the students were sceptical and

[10] *The Christian News-Letter*, December 11, 1940.
[11] *Atlantic Monthly*, February, 1942.

rowdies were plenty. . . . Most of the class before me were infidels and called each other Voltaire, Rousseau, D'Alembert, etc." It was predicted "that in two generations Christianity would altogether disappear." [12] It did not disappear, but the Christian movement among students has been one of the most vital and significant streams of influence both in this country and around the world. It is so today, despite its numerical weakness in the midst of a system of higher education which is beset by the problems of mass production. Nevertheless, even a casual conversation with a group of college students who have grown up in American churches reveals an abysmal ignorance concerning the nature of the religion to which they have been exposed, and with which many of them have nominally identified themselves.

If it is true that this is not a unique situation from a historical viewpoint, there are some features to our contemporary predicament which are unique. The world's need for Christianity is unique. The strength of the appeal which rival religions have for youth across the world is unique. The defection to other religions of great nations which have heretofore been in the main stream of Christian history is unique. The pressure of a secular civilization upon the mind of man is unique. The geographical extent of the war now enveloping the world is unique, and the spiritual demands of the problems arising out of the war are sure to be unique. It does not therefore seem to be an exaggeration to say that the teaching function of the church has assumed a unique importance in this age.

[12] *Autobiography and Correspondence of Lyman Beecher,* p. 43. Quoted by Henry B. Wright in *Two Centuries of Christian Activity at Yale,* p. 48.

The pastor's effectiveness as an educator will depend in part upon his ability to keep himself teachable. When Joseph Noyes was the minister of the First Church of New Haven, which the students of the newly transplanted Yale College were compelled to attend on penalty of a fine of twenty shillings per absence, President Clap once remonstrated with him on the ground that his preaching was not more edifying. "You do not know," replied Mr. Noyes, referring to the students and faculty of the college, "what an ignorant people I have to preach to." "Yes, I do," replied President Clap, "and I know that as long as you preach to them in this way they will always be ignorant." [13] Every minister, both in the pulpit and in his pastoral work, is tempted to attribute his failures to the stony soil on which he casts the seed, forgetting that he has a responsibility for preparing the ground as well as for sowing seed, and that he needs constantly to be learning how other people have succeeded in dealing with the very kind of soil with which he has had limited results. It is sometimes said among specialists in religious education that one of their most difficult problems is the education of pastors to understand education. True or false, such observations remind us that the only safety for those who teach others lies in being themselves very teachable.

In most churches it devolves upon the pastor to interpret to the congregation the importance of the church's educational opportunity. There will be a restricted group who understand that for potential usefulness nothing that the church can do compares with its educational work, if it is well done. Few church members would challenge that state-

[13] Leonard Bacon, *Thirteen Historical Discourses*, p. 240. Quoted by H. B. Wright, *Ibid.*, p. 32.

ment, but many would never give it much thought unless it were brought to their attention. It is the pastor's responsibility so to focus attention upon the educational function of the church. Not only is he the man who can most effectively persuade a congregation of the importance of this aspect of the church's work, so that it will receive adequate financial and personal support, but he is in a strategic position to interpret to the congregation what the Church School and other educational enterprises are doing. Unless he has an unusual congregation, these activities will need some interpretation. The methods of teaching employed today in all public and private schools are so different from those used forty years ago that it is impossible to secure the cooperation of boys and girls in Church School classes which are conducted along the methods of the earlier time, even if it were desirable to do so. There has come about a great change in Church School methods everywhere, and in some churches revolutionary change. This is not always understood by the laity of the church, or even by some of the people who are enlisted as teachers and workers in the church's educational program. Even where a church can have a Director of Religious Education to guide the formulation of policy, it is the pastor of the church who must take the lead in securing the enthusiastic cooperation of the whole congregation in these policies. It is also his task to help the congregation to understand that the church's educational program includes more than the Church School and Young People's Societies, important as they are. When in a town of forty-two thousand people, over a thousand adults are enrolled in the regular curriculum courses of the Adult Education Center, a church is out of touch with reality which does not make some provision for the religious education of adults as well as of youth. A congregation ought to think of itself as continually engaged in the process of educating itself in the deeper and larger meanings of Christian faith and life. If the pastor does not so interpret the congregation to itself, it is not likely to think of the church very often as an educational institution.

It may be the pastor's function to emphasize neglected aspects of the church's teaching opportunity. When the educational headlines are given to the creative function of the teacher, who is to remind the church that there is a Christian tradition which has been received and which must be handed on, a tradition which has itself been spiritually creative in many generations? When the Church School attempts the impossible task of trying in one hour a week through activities to build habits of Christian living to counteract the habits which all the rest of the week has built up, who is to suggest that there is still value in storing the mind with the Scriptures and that even in one hour a week a good deal can be accomplished, through activities and by other methods, along that line? When the educational process forgets that boys and girls come out of homes, and that they reflect the frustrations and tensions and hopes and fears which dominate those homes, who knows those homes well enough to understand the relationship between the child's problem and the home's problems? When a church becomes a discordant medley of groups carrying on a variety of educational projects, sometimes in rivalry with each other, or at least out of touch with each other, who is responsible for taking the lead in gathering up these disjointed efforts into some kind of unity? When the thoroughly wholesome emphasis upon Christian nurture is caricatured into the assumption that there is some educational process through which growing life can be passed with the assurance that it will be turned out at the end in the form of mature Christian character, who is to plead for the place of the will in all education, and to argue that there must be clear-cut decisions made by the individual at many points all along the line? These are not the exclusive obligations of the pastor, of course. But if he is fortunate enough not to be too deeply enmeshed in the detailed administration of the educational work of the church, he can render an invaluable service if from a somewhat objective viewpoint he keeps stressing aspects of the educational opportunity which may for the time being be neglected.

It is sometimes argued that a minister is by nature and by force of circumstances a propagandist rather than an educator. If the word propaganda is used in an invidious sense as meaning the proclamation of half-truths or untruths for questionable purposes, the criticism is so wide of the mark as to deserve no discussion. But that is not what is usually meant by this observation. It is made sometimes by very sincere people who think of the minister as one who proclaims with all the ardor of his being convictions in which he passionately believes, while the educator is one who sets out with a group of fellow-students on a calm, cold-minded dispassionate search for a truth which none of them, teacher or taught, has yet found. It is this conception of education which leads some people to maintain that the very nature of the minister's calling disqualifies him as an educator. But is this the whole truth about education? Is it not true that there is a need in all education for two attitudes toward truth: on the one hand, the attitude of research, which, setting aside every preconception and prejudice, embarks upon a thoroughly impartial and unemotional hunt for facts; and on the other, the attitude of teaching, which enthusiastically and confidently commends to inquiring minds the results of research which hold promise for human life? It is not often that these two attitudes are combined in equal measure in one person. The pastor who is a preacher will inevitably be, in a good sense, more of a propagandist than a laboratory man. But he is not thereby ruled out from a place of usefulness in education.

Dr. John Erskine once commented on the educational theory implied in the statement that, "by an intelligent examination of modern times we may discover a satisfactory goal, an ideal, a faith." He said:

"I respect the effort, but I do not kindle to it. . . . A great ideal is not evolved by a popular vote, nor by a debate. Some one has to believe it first. If he believes it enough he will preach it. His disciples will spread it. Culture will then take care of itself." He pleaded for "a desirable kind of a college in which men with the creative passion for their subjects advocate those subjects to whatever youth will listen. The born historian will advocate history, the confirmed writer will advocate literature, the dedicated scientist will plead for his research. In comparison with such a group, teaching what with all their hearts they believe in, the average college of today must seem withered and cynical; and in comparison with them a college given chiefly to critical examination of the universe must seem a little barren. And if the teacher cannot set forth his subject with that degree of flame, let him find another job." [14]

The minister who feels that in order to be an educator he must leave young people in doubt as to whether or not the Christian gospel means anything to him has mistaken his calling. His deep conviction that Christ is the Way, the Truth and the Life, his eagerness to share with other people the life with God which is life's richest meaning for him, his confident conviction that the Christian way is the way of salvation for the world—these are his assets as a teacher. If he refrains from dogmatically imposing them upon other people who are honestly seeking for the truth, but as occasion offers "sets forth his subject" with the flame of a pure devotion to it, he will be a minister through whose pastoral activity as well as pulpit ministry God may speak the Word that is life.

VIII

One of the satisfactions of the pastoral side of the ministry is that the opportunities which it presents are not dependent upon the size of the community or the size of the church. The promoter who measures everything in numbers seldom makes a good pastor, for the achievements of the pastorate are beyond the calculations of mathematics. In many ways a man can be a better pastor if he does not have too large a pastoral responsibility. Washington Gladden wrote of a change of pastorate which he made in his early ministry: "It might have seemed that in removing from a suburb of the metropolis to a New England town of ten thousand inhabitants I had narrowed my field of influence; on the con-

[14] John Erskine, "A New Education," *Saturday Review of Literature*, July 2, 1932.

trary, it appeared to me that I had vastly extended it." [15]
What a man does with a pastorate depends more upon his
interests than upon his environment. Is he interested in
wide ranges of life? Lord Tweedsmuir wrote of Sir Walter
Scott that, "he stood at the heart of life, and his interests
embraced everything that interested his fellows." [16] That is
where the pastor ought to stand. Is the pastor interested in
people, not as psychological specimens but as persons? No
pastoral relationship is possible without that kind of friendly
interest. "Can one point out to people their mistakes, their
sins, their faults without hurting them?" Leo Tolstoy once
wrote in his diary. "There is a spiritual chloroform, and it
has long been known—always the same—love. . . . The soul
is such a sensitive creature that an operation performed on it
without the chloroform of love is never anything but in-
jurious." [17] A few months before his death, Alexander
Whyte wrote in pencil a postscript to An Appeal for Prayer
on Behalf of Ireland. It was 1919, when Irish troubles were
at high tide. The postscript might well be in every pastor's
study:

> "Truth often separates:
> Love always unites.
> 'Love me' says Augustine, 'and then say anything to me
>   and about me you like.'

And Richard Baxter's people were wont to say, 'We take
all things well from one who always and wholly loves us.' " [18]

[15] *Reminiscences*, p. 162.
[16] John Buchan, *Sir Walter Scott*, p. 355.
[17] Vladimir Tchertkoff, *Last Days of Tolstoy*, p. 135. Quoted
from Tolstoy's Diary, January 25, 1889.
[18] *Op. cit.*, p. 615.

Is the minister contagiously interested in the church? If he is not, he will kill rather than create interest in the church on the part of lay people. As a matter of fact the intensity of his interest in the church is likely to be in proportion to the intensity of his service to the church. Dr. John H. Jowett understood this when he said that many a man who says of some cause, "I began to lose interest in it, and so I gave it up" ought rather to say, "I began to give it up, and then lost interest in it." [19] Is he deeply interested in religion? Of course he is interested in religion, or he would not be in the ministry. And yet there is a warning in George Tyrrell's description of "those who lose their religion by giving themselves to soul-absorbing labours in the cause of religion." [20] Is he interested in himself? Of course he is, and yet the more his life centers in Christ and the less it revolves around himself, the more help he can be to other people. Of a minister who has stood by his congregation in London thr ugh all that has befallen them, a mutual friend recently wrote, "He has had a harrowing two years, but his deep composure and willingness to divest himself of self-interest have brought him through." For such grace any pastor may well pray.

There is no aspect of a minister's varied activity in which he feels such kinship with his Master as he does when in touch with his people's needs as their pastor. He cannot imagine Jesus in surplice or gown preaching from a pulpit in an American church, deeply as he believes that this is what Jesus would want him to do. When he attends ecclesiastical gatherings he wonders sometimes whether Jesus would think

[19] *Things That Matter Most*, p. 126.

[20] M. D. Petre, *Autobiography and Life of George Tyrrell*, Vol. I, p. 109.

it necessary to spend quite so much time on the machinery of the church and so little on hard thinking concerning the church's duty and the church's opportunity. When he sees the neatly serried ranks in which even democratic churches divide the great from the less-great, he sometimes asks himself half-seriously, "What place would be given in that processional to a Carpenter?" When he tries to serve his community, he cannot help puzzling over the strange way in which every path of service winds somewhere to a committee-table, where he finds it hard to picture the Man of Nazareth. But when the pastor visits the homes of his congregation, wrestles with the difficulties of the people who come to him for help, tries to fuse together a diversified company of people into a fellowship, teaches by the curb-side and wherever inquirers are gathered together, challenges adults who are engrossed in their own affairs by putting a child in their midst—then the pastor knows that he is in a feeble way trying to do the very things that Jesus did in his matchless way. And though the pastor knows his limitations for the high and delicate tasks committed to him, he dares to pray that some day, when he is not aware of what is happening, as he is faithful to those tasks, God will speak His word to needy men.

VI

THE WORD AND WORSHIP

"And he saith unto me, These are true sayings of God. And I fell at his feet to worship him. And he said unto me, See thou do it not: I am thy fellowservant and of thy brethren that have the testimony of Jesus: worship God."

REVELATION 19:10

THE WORD AND WORSHIP

ONE of the clearly defined trends in the Christian church today is a revival of interest in the art of public worship. It is a revival, for there has never been a time in Christian history when corporate worship was not a central feature of the church's life. Pliny's famous letter and Justin Martyr's description of a Christian gathering make it plain that at least by the second century forms of public worship had been developed.[1] The aftermath of the Day of Pentecost, as it is described in the second chapter of the Book of Acts, would indicate that customary ways of practicing the presence of God had become habitual in the church at an even earlier date. "They continued steadfastly in the apostles' doctrine and fellowship, and in breaking of bread and in prayers." Teaching, fellowship, the eucharist and corporate prayer have continued to this day to be essential elements in the services of most churches. There have been times and places in which it has been felt that Christian worship should express spontaneously the mood and aspirations of the moment. At other times and in other fellowships worship has been more rigidly formalized, and emphasis has been laid upon the inspirations which come from knowing that the church in many places and at many times has approached God through the very words in use at the moment.

[1] *Ante-Nicene Fathers;* Vol. I *Apostolic Fathers, Justin Martyr and Irenæus,* pp. 185-6.
Letter of Pliny the Younger, Governor of Bithynia, to Trajan, 112 A.D., quoted by Shirley J. Case, *The Historicity of Jesus,* pp. 242-4.

Whether through liturgy or the free stirrings of the spirit, the church has always been a worshipping fellowship, and at the heart of its life has been the faith that when men sincerely worship Him God communicates His Word to them.

The primary importance of worship is revealed by the fact that although the church has done many different things at different periods, it has always been a worshipping fellowship. Worship is not the only continuing function in the life of the church. It has always, with some exceptions, been a preaching church. It has always, again with rare exceptions, engaged in works of mercy. It has nearly always been a missionary church. But always it has been a nucleus of activities that issued from a central act of worship. It is sometimes argued that the act of worship is of greater significance than the activities that flow from it. The Archbishop of Canterbury, certainly not indifferent to the social message of the church, has said that "the most effective thing that the church of Christ can do in the world, and the most effective thing that any individual Christian can do is to lift up his heart in adoration to God. . . . Adoration, the utter giving of the self to God that he might fill it, a total forgetfulness of self in the presence of God that God may be all and in all—that is the heart of worship." [2] Arguments as to which is the more important, worship or life, are not very productive. It is like debating the relative value of a tree and its fruit, when both are necessary parts of one whole. It may fairly be said, however, that the Protestant church is frequently in danger of minimizing the importance of worship, thus endangering its own soul and impoverishing its fruitage.

[2] William Temple, *Basic Convictions*, pp. 19-20.

II

There are clearly discernible reasons why the Protestant church has sometimes looked with suspicion upon the development of worship, or if not suspicious has at least been neglectful of this aspect of the church's ministry. In recent years there has been in some quarters a fear that the church might turn to worship as an escape from the rigorous demands of the social ethic that is implicit in the Christian gospel. That an interest in worship may be used as such an escape is obvious. That it ought to be and can be an incentive to social effort has been demonstrated by such diverse groups as the Guild of St. Matthew in the Anglican Church, with a rich liturgical form of worship, and the Society of Friends, whose worship follows a pattern of utter simplicity. There has also been a distrust of formal worship in Protestant churches based on the fear that there may be an inherent contradiction between sincerity and form. That is a healthy fear. Sincerity is the first essential in all worship of the God of truth, and the moment any service becomes tainted with a suggestion of showmanship, its reality is gone. There is a tendency in some non-liturgical churches to introduce forms of worship taken over from other traditions without careful analysis of what those forms mean and how they can honestly be used. The result sometimes is a hodge-podge of liturgical forms bound together by no central thread of meaning, and moving in no perceptible direction. But sincerity is a quality of the spirit, not the property of a particular form of worship. A minister can read a prayer in public worship with complete sincerity, or he can offer extemporaneous prayer while his heart is far away. The important matter is that whatever he

does should be done with clear intention, after the discipline
of thought and study, as the expression of a dedicated spirit.
Then let him find whatever form seems to him to be appropriate to this highest and noblest exercise of intellect and
emotion.

Worship is sometimes undervalued because people have
been disappointed in its immediate results. George Eliot
represented Romola as finding in a simple act of human kindness the faith which she could not experience on her knees:

"Calmness would not come even on the altar steps; it
would not come from looking at the serene picture where the
saint, writing in the rocky solitude, was being visited by
faces with celestial peace in them. Romola was in the hard
press of human difficulties; and that rocky solitude was too
far off. She rose from her knees that she might hasten to
her sick people in the courtyard, and by some immediate
beneficent action revive that sense of worth in life which
at this moment was unfed by any wider faith." [3] But the
reality of worship is not to be tested by its immediate emotional results. Its effect on our wills is much more important
than its influence on our feelings. Both in the realm of
volition and feeling its influence is not discernible so much
in the isolated instance as in the general direction and quality
of the life inspired by it. In the last analysis its ultimate
validity depends not upon human judgments as to its results
but upon its value to God.

The great heresy of modern churchmanship is the notion
that the busiest church and the noisiest church is necessarily
the most productive church. But a church can be very busy
about the wrong things, or about trivial matters, and it can

[3] George Eliot, *Romola.*

make a great hubbub about nothing at all. In an age which respects rush and often mistakes sound for sense, it is perhaps not strange that the mood of worship should be unknown to many people, as it undoubtedly is.

Many moderns do not worship because they do not know what worship is. "Worship," says Evelyn Underhill, "is the total adoring response of man to the One Eternal God self-revealed in time." [4] It is a total response. As Archbishop Temple has put it:

"It calls for all your faculties. It is the use of your mind to work out the revelation of himself that God has given. It is the opening of your imagination that it may be filled with pictures of his glory and of his love. It is the submission of your conscience that it may be quickened and enlightened by his perfect holiness. It is, because of all these, the subjugation of your will, that he may take you and use you. And you become glad to be used even though you cannot see the purpose for which he is doing it. Sometimes he lets us know but often not. What we should be sure of is that if we truly open our hearts and submit our wills to him, he is working his purpose through us whether or not we ever come to know it." [5] Not knowing what worship is, or what to expect from the practice of worship, many people simply do not worship, even when they come to church.

III

It is sometimes said that the aridity of Protestant worship is due to an over-emphasis on preaching. It would be truer to the facts to say that sometimes both preaching and wor-

[4] *Worship*, p. 61.
[5] *Basic Convictions*, p. 20.

ship miss the mark because the relationship between them is imperfectly understood. If the preacher thinks of a service of worship as a device by which he can create an atmosphere in which he can preach effectively, any reality which that service of worship may have will be either accidental or providential. It will be another evidence that God can retrieve the mistakes of those who are called to be His servants. Every minister must decide whether the service of worship is a preparation for the sermon (there are legitimate ways in which the service of worship may be so considered as a preparation for the sermon by those who hold that the sermon is the supreme channel through which the Word of God comes to men), or whether the service and the sermon are equal parts of one total act of worship in which the church is engaged. A minister who is conducting public worship ought to be clear in his own mind as to what the relationship between these two major parts of a church service is.

Whatever his view, it ought not to be said as one minister reports his people as saying, that "the service of worship lifts us up, and then the sermon lets us down." On any theory, the sermon should be for the congregation a creative experience in which they know themselves to be in the presence of God. Therefore the sermon cannot arrive at God at the end of an argument, or at the end of a meandering process not to be dignified by the name of argument, nor can references to God be arbitrarily thrust into the concluding paragraph of a sermon where they seem ill at ease and out of place, but the whole sermon must be lived in the presence of God whether the references to Him be explicit or implicit. Some continuity of thought between the service of worship and the sermon helps to bind the two together into one bundle of life. This continuity should not be so pronounced as to become monotony. Worship moves through a variety of moods, and if every hymn and every prayer center too directly in the same thought, the service as a whole loses a richness which it may rightfully claim. And yet if the sermon deals with a large theme the worship of the hour will naturally voice aspirations, thanksgivings, and confessions which come within the same orbit. If a sermon deals exclusively in analysis, if it scolds or luxuriates in denunciation, if it is purely descriptive in its dealing with the Christian life, or if it opens no windows onto a world unseen, it is very likely to constitute a break in the hour of worship. If, however, the sermon links the worshipper with his Christian heritage in the Bible and the church, if it keeps constantly in touch both with "the timely and the timeless," if it lays hold on the worshipper so that as he listens he makes his response not to the preacher but to God whose Word finds the worshipper through the sermon, then legitimately it may be said that the sermon is not distinct from the church's act of worship but is a living part of that worship.

IV

The conduct of public worship is, of course, an art, and requires on the part of those who are engaged in it the intellectual and spiritual discipline which every art demands of its practitioners. It is, according to Percy Dearmer, "the most neglected of the arts . . . the most comprehensive and the most difficult of the arts." [6] Let the philosophers wrestle with the problems involved in the relationship of art and

[6] In the *Spectator* (London), September 28, 1934.

religion. The minister knows that just as thoughtful men will always try to find appropriate ways of expressing great ideas, emotions, and loyalties, so he must worthily express through worship the convictions, feelings, and devotion which are religion. His need for an art of worship is intensified by the fact that a leader of public worship is something more than a man saying his prayers in public. He is called to the delicate task of enlisting the minds, consciences, aspirations, and wills of a heterogeneous collection of people in one corporate act of dedication. He must speak for them in the offices he undertakes, and he must make it possible for them in their hearts to be at one with him as he addresses the Most High God on their behalf. So august a proceeding is not to be approached thoughtlessly or carelessly. It demands and deserves the best that the minister can give it out of his thought and life. As Dr. William E. Orchard has put it: "Although spontaneity in prayer should be our aim; just as in the case of a musician, brilliant execution is only secured by practice of scales, or extemporization by knowing the rules of harmony and studying the great masters; so, in prayer, the simplest way to spontaneity is a basis of order." [7] If he has the gifts which are necessary to invest the act with beauty, he may honestly regard the consecrated exercise of those gifts as part of the spiritual sacrifice which he lays upon the altar. He must not degrade the act of worship by seizing it as an opportunity to display himself or whatever gifts he may possess. A public prayer becomes a kind of profanity when those who are asked to engage in it are more conscious of its phrases than of its meaning, and suspect that while

[7] *The Way of Simplicity*, p. 222.

the minister is asking them to unite with him in prayer, he
is at the same time half-unconsciously inviting them to ad-
mire the literary skill with which he prays. The remedy for
showmanship, however, is not the careless spontaneity which
saunters unprepared into the presence of God, but is such
dedication of every skill to God as removes from its exercise the taint of self-consciousness and self-display. Is not
that essential to truth in every art?

> "The hand that rounded Peter's dome,
>   And groined the aisles of Christian Rome,
>   Wrought in a sad sincerity;
>   Himself from God he could not free;
>   He builded better than he knew;—
>   The conscious stone to beauty grew." [8]

The art of worship does not consist in spectacular buildings,
showy music, "light effects," ritual innovations, or theatrical
conduct on the part of the clergy. It does mean the conscientious use of every medium at the church's disposal to lift
men's minds toward God who is the Author of Beauty, the
Source of Truth, the Fountain of Goodness, and to unite
a worshipping congregation in a common dedication of every
power to Him, who is the Giver of every gift. The conduct
of such corporate worship is the highest of the arts, and all
who have tried to thread their way among its hazards and
pitfalls would agree that it is among the most difficult.

V

If the Protestant church is to make the worship of God
the center of its life, it is obvious that the people of the

[8] Ralph W. Emerson, *The Problem.*

churches must understand better than they now do what they may legitimately expect when the habit of worship is woven into the pattern of their lives. It is true that when we approach worship from the standpoint of what we can get out of it, we are likely to get nothing out of it except disappointment. It is of the essence of worship that we leave off trying to use God for our purposes, and offer ourselves to Him to be used by Him for His purposes. Such self-offering, however, does have results in the life of the devotee which are pitifully misunderstood by multitudes of church people, who think of church going as a duty, welcome or unwelcome according to the entertainment value of minister and choir, or who imagine that the worship of God has reality only for people of mystical temperament who stand somewhat apart from the workaday world.

An interpretation of what worship can mean to ordinary people is one of the needs of the day. It can help them to make life whole. "We need it," wrote Dr. Richard Cabot, "to cure us of absorption in the fragment, to free it from lonely isolation." [9] Worship helps men to achieve freedom. Three thinkers as diverse as Henri Bergson,[10] Henry N. Wieman,[11] and William Ernest Hocking,[12] have in recent times pointed out that when man worships, he, who is ordinarily a creature of habits, escapes from the grooves in which his life has settled down, and starts cutting out new channels along which his life can move. Worship enhances the creative powers of the individual.

[9] *What Men Live By*, p. 273.
[10] *The Two Sources of Morality and Religion*, pp. 216-17.
[11] *Religious Experience and Scientific Method*, p. 130.
[12] *Meaning of God in Human Experience*, pp. 363-5.

> "Here is a quiet room!
> Pause for a little space;
> And in the deepening gloom,
> With hands before thy face,
> Pray for God's grace.
>
> Pray for the strength of God,
> Strength to obey His plan;
> Rise from your knees less clod
> Than when your prayer began,
> More of a man." [13]

To enable the worshipper to be "less clod" and to become "more of a man" is one of the distinctive results of worship, whether that development take place suddenly or by that slower growth which Phillips Brooks described when he said: "There comes a culture out of this religious life. From the silent Bible reading, from the heart's meeting with the wonders of the life divine, there comes a trueness and fineness, a manliness and a womanliness that courts never give." [14] Worship releases people from strain. "How can it possibly fail," said William James, "to cool the fever, appease the fret, and steady the nerves if one is sensibly conscious that his life as a whole and not as a part is in the keeping of One whom he can absolutely trust?" [15] Worship helps us to see ourselves and our tasks in a new perspective. As an artist looks away from his work and then back at it

[13] Donald Cox, A *Treasury of Prayers and Praises for Use in Toc H*, p. 21.

[14] A. V. G. Allen, *Life and Letters of Phillips Brooks*, Vol. I, p. 253.

[15] William James, quoted by John G. McKenzie, in *Personal Problems of Conduct and Religion*, p. 144.

to see it more clearly, as the traveller returns from his journey to see familiar scenes with fresh vision, as one who has heard great music always thereafter measures all sounds by a new standard, so the man who has lifted his eyes to God in sincerity and truth always sees familiar things against the background of a divinely beneficent Purpose for all men. Worship corrects our sense of direction.

> "Where lies the land to which the ship would go?
> Far, far ahead, is all her seamen know." [16]

But the man who worships sets his compass by the magnetic pole. Worship renews dynamic for life. "What it did for her she never knew," wrote Margaret Prescott Montague of a hard pressed woman who kept a picture of Christ in a bureau drawer to which she could turn when she seemed to be at the end of her resources. "She only knew that she was in the presence of something transcendent, something that touched the deepest thing in her." [17] So she renewed the springs of her life in solitary worship. Worship through which men and women in companies bow before their common Father is mankind's supreme affirmation of social solidarity. "There is no savour like that of bread shared between men,"[18] writes Antoine de Saint Exupèry about the breaking of bread in a French peasant's home near Arras, and the reader's mind turns as though drawn by a magnet to the sharing of the Bread of Life in the Eucharist which lifts human fellowship into a divine partnership. Dr. Herbert

[16] Arthur Hugh Clough, *Where Lies the Land*.
[17] Margaret Prescott Montague, "The Will to Go," *Atlantic Monthly*, May, 1921.
[18] *Flight to Arras*, p. 212.

Gray once said that experiences of the reality of God had been for him "not highly emotional but rather quiet and harmonizing, bringing with them a sense of being rightly adjusted at last to the universe and the people in it." [19] If the Word of God is to come with power to worshipping congregations, they must be helped to understand these simple ways in which God speaks to those who worship Him.

Protestant churches, however, need also to remember that it is the church's faith that our worship has value to God. Whether its primary value is to God or to man is a question which only God can answer. The energy which goes into the debates concerning the relative importance of the subjective and objective values in worship could perhaps be more constructively employed. We *know* that worship has demonstrable values to us. We *believe* that our worship has value to God. As a matter of fact, all the subjective values in worship would disappear, and every act of worship would become an empty sham, if we did not believe that it means something to God. A man may practice autosuggestion for the sake of its effect upon his own mind, but he cannot worship God because he knows that he will feel better after he has done so. Let us then be content to affirm our faith that worship is man's response to God who meets man as he worships, with beneficent results for the worshipper. If worship is a response, and not a trick of man's invention, it must mean something to God since He takes the initiative in calling out the response. That He does take such initiative seems clear. There is in man an impulse to worship which man did not contrive because he thought that it would help him to get along in the world. It

[19] *Finding God*, p. 29.

seems to be as natural for a man to worship as it is for him
to breathe or sleep or eat or let his eye linger on a lovely
landscape. Call it man's attempt to adjust himself to his
spiritual environment if you will, and the fact still remains
that man does not create his spiritual environment. It is
given, and it calls to man—or God calls through it. Can the
Christian faith be wrong when it affirms that God is seeking
fellowship with men? Is not life more and more the pressure
upon our life of a Larger Life seeking our cooperation for
ends that are better and broader than the measure of our
minds? Why? That is the abiding mystery. But the fact
seems clear.

Of course there are multitudes of people who are not aware
of any such need for correspondence with the larger life of
God. That is partly due to the fact that our man-made civilization occupies so much of the horizon. George Borrow observed in his *Bible in Spain* that he had always "found in
the disposition of the children of the fields a more determined tendency to religion and piety than amongst the inhabitants of towns and cities." The reason, he thought, was
obvious. It was because they were in closer touch with
superhuman realities, and because their work was "less favor-
able to the engendering of self-conceit and sufficiency, so
utterly at variance with that lowliness of spirit which constitutes the best foundation of piety." [20] It is doubtful if
there is more piety in rural regions today than in cities. At
least it is not hard to find countrysides which once were
more productive of faith than of crops which have now
relapsed into a near-paganism, or at least have become
thoroughly unchurched. There is, however, no country dis-

[20] *The Bible in Spain*, pp. 15-6.

trict in America which has not absorbed the machine age, with its emphasis upon human ingenuity and its forgetfulness of divine power. Even more deadening to the spirit than the delusion of man's omnipotence is the acquisitive temper which has dominated modern life. Multitudes of people are not aware of the possibility of fellowship with God, because that is not what they supremely want. And yet, even for the most secular-minded and the most possessive, there are times when the things on which the heart has been set turn to dust and ashes, and the man who did not know he believed in God finds his soul crying out for God!

Man makes his response in varied ways to the God who seeks his fellowship. All honest work, all fashioning of beauty, all unveiling of truth, all ministries of kindness, all linking of human hands in understanding, forge the bonds of partnership between men and their God who seeks to work through men both to will and to do of His good pleasure. But that fellowship, inarticulate and dimly apprehended in so many ranges of human thought and action, becomes most articulate and most delightful when man gathers up all his conscious life in adoration of the Beauty and Power and Love of God. Adoration is not pragmatic in intention. It is the appropriate response of the creature to the Creator, of sinful man to Holy God, of the lonely human to the God who for reasons that the human cannot fathom cares about the man who adores. Put it simply—if God be Our Father, the articulate response that we make to His love is of moment to Him. It is a caricature of Christian worship to say that it is based on belief in a God who wants to be flattered. It is shallow flippancy to say (as has

been said in our time) that God must be bored by the endless singing of His praises. The voicing of honest loyalty is
not flattery, and it is only loveless fellowship that is boring.
So long as God calls men to be fellow-workers with Himself,
and in their sharing of His purposes gives Himself to them,
so long we may believe with confidence that the act of worship which is life to our spirits has its larger meanings in
the life of God.

VI

Christian worship therefore begins with the contempla-
tion of the greatness of God. "I saw the Lord high and lifted
up," [21] says Isaiah. In some sense that is the initial step in
all true worship. We look beyond the work of our own
hands and beyond the world as it is, with all its wonder
and all its horror, to Him who was before all worlds and
who will be when all worlds that He has created have
crumbled to dust.

> "O come, let us worship and bow down:
> Let us kneel before the Lord our Maker.
> For He is our God;
> And we are the people of His pasture,
> And the sheep of His hand.
> It is He that hath made us, and not we ourselves." [22]

Mr. G. K. Chesterton has written somewhere that "it must
be an exhilarating experience that they enjoy who suggest
amendments to this universe as it seems determined to conduct itself. To think that they could have made the world

[21] Isaiah 6:1.
[22] Psalm 95:6-7; 100:3.

so much better than it is must be an uplifting reflection. But it must be for that very reason a devastating reflection if it should ever occur to them to realize that they could not have made the world at all." [23] Worship begins in that realization that we are creatures looking up to our Creator. This is the truth which Baron Friedrich von Hugel contended for so stoutly when Christianity was teetering on the edge of humanism. "We shall ever have to look up to God," he wrote to Clement Webb, "to apprehend, not comprehend Him. . . . We are not, and never will be God." [24] To George Tyrrell he wrote, "If one were to take your clear-cut Immanentism as final and complete, that noblest half of the religious experience, of tip-toe expectation, of unfulfilled aspiration, of a sense of a divine life, of which our own but touches the outskirts, would have no place." President Arthur T. Hadley once remarked that many ministers seemed to forget that it was Almighty God whom they were addressing in their public prayers. Remembering that fact is the point at which genuine worship takes its start.

But worship does not end on that exalted plane. No honest man can contemplate the holiness of God without a fresh and vivid awareness of his own unholiness. Christian worship is permeated throughout by the contrast between infinite God and finite man, the righteousness of God and the sinfulness of man, the sufficiency of God and the need of man, the self-giving of God and the supplication of man. The worshipper is always

[23] Quoted by John A. Hutton in *The British Weekly* (unidentified).

[24] *Letters of Baron Friedrich von Hugel*, pp. 138-9.

> "Man, poor elf
> Striving to match the finger-mark of Him
> The immeasurably matchless." [25]

Worship moves on two planes at the same time. It is not merely that a service of worship begins naturally with invocation of the divine presence, and then moves inevitably to confession of human creaturehood and human sin. The two notes are heard like point and counterpoint with recurring emphasis throughout the period of worship. If worship dwells exclusively or too long upon the majesty of God, it loses touch with the ground on which the worshipper's feet must walk. If it dwells with excessive insistence upon the inadequacy and failure which are the marks of human life, it becomes mere introspection and loses its hold on God. Worship is a ladder set between heaven and earth, and the worshipper must be aware of both relationships throughout his devotions. Here again Dr. Orchard comes to our aid: "Prayer," he says, "marks the very turning-point at which man acknowledges his nature and yet looks beyond it; realizes his need and recognizes that God alone can help him; his mind has been awakened by the light, he turns his eyes gladly towards it, he stretches out his hands, he calls on God." [26] So with all worship. "I beheld the Lord high and lifted up . . . Then said I, I am a man of unclean lips, and I dwell in the midst of a people of unclean lips." When the sense of the everlasting contrast between God and man fades out of worship, it becomes either aestheticism or sentimentalism but not fellowship.

[25] Robert Browning, *With Francis Furini.*
[26] Wm. E. Orchard, *The Way of Simplicity*, p. 212.

If worship is to be the expression of existing fellowship between God and man, the personal note must be maintained in the forms of worship. Worship is not merely quiet meditation about life and its problems, although such meditation may enter into it. Worship is addressed to Some One who is supremely worthy of man's highest praise and deepest loyalty. Facing facts and trying to see what one can make of them is a valuable exercise, but it is not worship. Christian worship consists in the facing of One Central Fact —the fact of God as He has been revealed in Christ. The definition of that relationship between man and God has always been too much for the limited capacities of language. "Art Thou not it?" [27] asked Isaiah in a momentary confusion of language which probably betrayed the confusion at that moment in his mind. He could not speak of God as less than a person, for then he could not speak to Him at all. And yet the terms ordinarily used to describe personal relationships were obviously inadequate, for God is beyond all the limitations with which time and space, ignorance and sin circumscribe humanity. Since language is necessarily unable to hold the whole truth about God, man who must express himself in words will perforce use the most capacious words at his disposal when he speaks about God. He will not try to pull God down to the level of things by using impersonal terms. God is "He," not "it," although He is beyond our understanding, and His ways are past our finding out. We use the personal pronoun for God, not because we attribute to God the limitations of personality, but because we have no other words at our command that lead us into any richer ranges of experience. In worship, however,

[27] Isaiah 51:9, 10.

we shift from the third person pronoun to the second. "Worship," says Dr. Hocking, "intends to institute some communication or transaction with God wherein will answers will . . . We recognize here an other-than-theoretical relation . . . which is seen quite simply in that transition in consciousness from 'he' to 'thou', and from 'thou' to 'we.' " [28] Too much of our modern worship remains in the third person, on the assumption that God is sub-personal rather than super-personal. In Christian worship every art should be employed to say to the hesitant spirit that shrinks from the audacity of addressing God,

> "Speak to Him thou for He hears,
>   And Spirit with Spirit can meet—" [29]

Does that seem too presumptuous? Not when we remember Jesus' instruction, "When ye pray, say Our Father."

VII

If worship is always a "two-way passage" between God and man, it involves on the part of the worshipper both receiving and giving. St. Paul quotes Jesus as having said, when and where we do not know, "It is more blessed to give than to receive." [30] It may be more blessed, but sometimes receiving is harder than giving. Specifically, it is easier for activist Americans to give themselves to a cause than it is for them to receive the inspirations and the guidance which they need in choosing their cause. Evelyn Underhill was right in saying that we spend our lives for the most part "conjugating

[28] *Meaning of God in Human Experience*, pp. 341, 343.
[29] Alfred Tennyson, *The Higher Pantheism*.
[30] Acts 20:35.

three verbs: to Want, to Have, and to Do . . . forgetting
that none of these verbs have any ultimate significance, except so far as they are transcended by and included in, the
fundamental verb, to Be." [31] "So many Christians are like
deaf people at a concert. They study the programme carefully, believe every statement made in it, speak respectfully
of the quality of the music, but only really hear a phrase now
and again. So they have no notion at all of the mighty symphony which fills the universe, to which our lives are destined to make their tiny contribution, and which is the self-
expression of the Eternal God." [32]

Let us not be intimidated by the limitations of our vocabulary when it comes to recognizing the reality of worshipful
receptivity. Inevitably we speak of worship in terms of *hear-
ring, seeing, feeling,* all of them words which describe functions of the physical senses. No doubt there are mystics
whose experience in worship is so vivid that it can hardly be
distinguished from psychophysical reactions. But there are
multitudes of worshippers for whom this is not so. They
do not see visions, or hear voices, or experience emotional
thrills when they worship. And yet they are sure that something of incalculable worth is given to them in the presence
of God. They are more alive on the highest levels of life
because they have received vitality from Him. Henry
Thoreau said that he went to Walden Pond, "because I
wished to live deliberately, to front only the essential facts
of life, and see if I could not learn what it had to teach, and
not when I came to die, discover that I had not lived. I did

[31] *The Spiritual Life,* p. 24.
[32] *Ibid.,* pp. 18-9.

not wish to live what was not life, living is so dear." [33] That
is a universal need. Is it not true that people discover a new
height and depth to life through what comes to their worshipping spirits? New quickness of sympathy, new strength
of resolution, new confidence before the unknown, new
clarity of purpose, new assurance of a Will encountered in
all of life but consciously confronted in this waiting moment—these gifts do not come when striven for but through
"a wise passiveness." Marius the Epicurean saw a band of
Christian men "who had faced life and were glad," because
"there was a cleansing and kindling flame at work in them
which made everything else that Marius had ever known
look comparatively vulgar and mean." [34] They had received
that renewal of life which is one side of worship.

But receiving cannot be separated from self-giving which
is the other side of worship. Some one has defined worship,
perhaps too exclusively and yet with insight, as "the giving of one's self to something greater than one's self by
which one is lifted out of one's self." [35] Mr. Justice Benjamin N. Cardozo said to the students at the Jewish Institute
of Religion a decade ago: "The submergence of self in the
pursuit of an ideal, the readiness to spend oneself without
measure, prodigally, almost ecstatically, for something intuitively apprehended as great and noble, spend oneself
one knows not why—some of us like to believe that this is
what religion means." [36] Christian worship identifies that
"readiness to spend oneself without measure" with the

[33] Henry S. Canby in *Yale Review*, Spring, 1931.
[34] Walter Pater, *Marius the Epicurean*, II, p. 130.
[35] An anonymous article in *The Christian Century*, June, 1931.
[36] *The Christian Century*, June, 1931.

Cross of Christ. What laid hold of Walter Pater's Marius
was "the image of a young man giving up voluntarily, one
by one, for the greatest ends, the greatest gifts; actually
parting with himself, yet from the midst of his desolation,
crying out upon the greatness of his success, as if foreseeing
this very worship." [37] Worship as an act of Christian consecration is a response to the self-giving of Christ upon the
Cross. Thought, imagination, the appreciations, the desire
for fellowship, all have their part in it. But no act of worship is complete until the will also is enlisted, and the worshipper, having received a renewal of life in the inward man,
responds,

> "Thou gav'st Thy life for me,
> I give myself to Thee." [38]

At the heart of true worship is the sacrifice, and in Christian
worship it is the sacrifice of self to the purposes of God.
Worship without that becomes a mere show. William
James once wrote of Renan: "He used the vocabulary of
the moral and religious life too sweetly and freely for one
whose thought refused to be *bound* by those ideals. Moral
ideals go with refusals and sacrifices, and there is something
shocking about the merely *musical* function they play in
Renan's pages. So I call him *profoundly* superficial. But
what an artist!" [39] Worship as an art which leads to no sacrifice is like the lovely old bridge at Avignon, with one end
resting on a pillar in mid-stream, never reaching the farther
shore.

[37] *Op. cit.*, pp. 138-9.
[38] Frances R. Havergal.
[39] Ralph Barton Perry, *Life and Letters of William James*, Vol. II,
p. 252. Letter to Charles Ritter, October 5, 1892.

VIII

Sometimes it is the misuse of symbols which defeats the great ends at which the worship of the living God ought to arrive. Some use of symbolism in worship is inevitable. Worship must take place somewhere, and the physical setting in which the act of worship takes place is bound to point beyond itself to something. A garish chandelier, a sentimental window, an iron stove, a pitcher of water on the pulpit, a battered Bible, a dingy wall—any physical object within range of vision will carry the thoughts of worshippers to something, whether it be to the indolence of a sexton, the poverty of a treasury, the faithfulness of an office-holder, or to the majesty of God. How important it is that every place of worship should in some visible ways carry the mind out beyond the visible to the invisible glory of God! This can be done through simplicity as well as through an elaborate multiplicity of symbolic detail. A Friends' Meeting House can speak of God as convincingly as a cathedral. Furthermore, every service of worship includes some symbolic action. Ushers noisily greeting arrivals in the vestibule, the minister turning the pages of his hymnal in search of a hymn, members of the choir whispering to each other during the sermon, a congregation sitting in silence, the breaking of the bread and the taking of the cup—actions speak louder than words in every service, and draw the minds of those who have come to worship to the weaknesses of humanity, or remind them of the grace that was in Christ, or fuse them into a spirit of fellowship in God. How important it is that the actions should be directed to a great end, the adoration of the God who is the Lord of all being, yet near to every

loving heart! A sexton can dust a pulpit to the glory of
God, and a minister can open the Bible in a blasphemous
spirit of self-display. What the symbolic object or the symbolic action may be matters less than how it is used.

The first essential is that the leader in worship should know
what the symbols are intended to express. "Blessed art
thou if thou knowest what thou doest," is nowhere more
true than in dealing with the symbols of worship. Is it a
communion table or an altar at the center of the chancel?
Modern church architecture often makes it difficult for us
to know. Is an altar an ornamental piece of furniture or
a symbol of sacrifice? Again, we are often left in the dark.
Does the minister turn and face the altar because that is a
dramatic action or because he attributes some sanctity to the
altar not possessed by the pulpit? One often wonders. Does
a national flag in the chancel stand for a narrow nationalism
or for a nation dedicated to the universal brotherhood of
nations? It is very important for us in these times that we
should know. Is the cross a thing of magic, or does it tell
to all Christians the story of life gladly given for the world's
redemption? Our whole interpretation of the gospel may
depend upon our understanding of that symbol. Churches
of the liturgical tradition generally have their symbols designated for them by their rubrics. They have educated their
people in the meaning of the symbolism they employ. Non-
liturgical churches have in recent years been recovering for
their own use some of the symbols which were banished from
their sanctuaries at the time of the Reformation. Where
this is done with understanding and discrimination, these
symbols can be means of grace. Where they are employed
without understanding or interpretation, they may become

mere novelties that confuse and distract, failing utterly in
their purpose as mediators of the Word of God to men.
Every symbol is to be sacramentally used, as the outward
and visible sign of some inward and spiritual grace. The
leader in worship who is to discover that symbols can be
windows opening out onto wider realities rather than stum-
bling-blocks for the spirit, must know why he uses them,
what they mean to him, and what they can mean to people
who need visible as well as invisible reminders of the love of
God.

IX

The Christian church has a great heritage in its treasury
of prayers and praises through which generations of Christian
people have been helped to worship God. Some of these
ancient prayers are living links between the divided churches
of today and the undivided church of the early Christians.
The *Sursum Corda*, the oldest piece of liturgy of which we
know, probably originated before the fourth century. It is
as vital today as it was then.

> "Lift up your hearts.
> We lift them up unto the Lord.
> Let us give thanks unto our Lord God.
> It is meet and right so to do.

It is very meet, right and our bounden duty, that we should
at all times, and in all places, give thanks unto Thee, O Lord,
Holy Father, Almighty Everlasting God.

Therefore with Angels and Archangels, and with all the
company of heaven, we laud and magnify Thy glorious
name; evermore praising Thee, and saying,

Holy, Holy, Holy, Lord God of hosts,
Heaven and earth are full of Thy glory:
Glory be to Thee, O Lord Most High.   Amen."

This Eucharistic hymn was sung when early Christians broke
bread together with a sense of grateful wonder at the incom-
prehensible power and manifold grace of God. It is an almost perfect expression of the blended awe, thankfulness,
joy, and consecration which are the appropriate attitudes at
a communion service today. It voices the worship of the
universal church, and it belongs to the universal church.
We who are affiliated with churches which cast aside such
elements of our common heritage owe a great debt to those
churches which in their liturgies preserved and continued
to use these classic expressions of the human spirit worshipping the divine life and love of God. There is a wealth of
such aid to the spirit of aspiring man. We ought to avail
ourselves of it, insofar as we find it helpful.

In so doing, we must recognize very frankly that many
ancient prayers and some modern prayers are not helpful
when used today in public worship. Prayers which are
couched in language so archaic as to give them an antiquarian
interest rather than a contemporary significance are not helpful, at least to most of us. Prayers which are built around a
theological outlook which the congregation know is at variance with that held by their minister who leads them in
worship introduce confusion of thought into what ought to
be concentrated attention on one thought. Prayers in which
there is an obvious striving for literary effect rob worship
of the essential ingredient of complete sincerity. Prayers
through which the personality of the author is obtrusively

conspicuous are inappropriate for public worship. This is true whether the leader of worship is offering his own prayer or is using one composed by another. Every prayer used in corporate worship should have a communal quality. The worshipping group should feel that this is their prayer, voicing their longings and their faith, and should not be distracted from the high business in hand by the reflection that Dr. Blank is offering an eloquent petition. To be specific, James Martineau's great prayer beginning, "O God, who art and wast and art to come, before whose face the generations rise and pass away," [40] says what every genuine worshipper wants to say in words in which he can honestly say it, while many of the exquisite petitions in Thomas à Kempis's *Imitation of Christ* are too exquisite to come naturally to the lips or from the hearts of most people. At a time like our own when there is renewed appreciation of the church's devotional heritage, there is real danger that the indiscriminate use of fine prayers in modern services may become an obstacle rather than an aid to the spirit of worship. If, as he well may, the minister even in a traditionally non-liturgical church is to use in public worship ancient and modern prayers composed by others along with those of his own composition, let him choose those couched in simple, straightforward but dignified English, which come out of a theological background congenial with that of the people whom he leads, voicing aspirations and affirmations which are real to the people with whom he seeks to establish a spiritual unity in corporate worship.

That is not to say that the minister cannot make good use of the Christian literature of devotion, even where he finds

[40] James Martineau, *Home Prayers*, p. 104.

THE WORD AND WORSHIP

it unsuitable for his purposes in the services of the church. He can find it a stimulus to his own life of devotion, which must be real if he is to be a leader of the worship of others. There is not much in Lancelot Andrewes's *Preces Privatae* which could be used in a church service today, but there is a great deal that can feed the soul of a man embarking upon the hazards of leading church services today. From the long range point of view, there is nothing which can so safeguard a minister from banality and triviality in public prayer as constant association with *A Chain of Prayer Across the Ages*, to use the title of Selina F. Fox's magnificent anthology. Incidentally, the brooding over great prayers can do more than anything else to introduce into a minister's own prayers the unconscious rhythm, which when sought for in public prayer becomes an artifice, but which when spontaneous brings prayer into accord with the great rhythms of life, which seem to be inherent in the purposes of God. In his immediate tasks of preparation for services of worship, a minister can find helpful allies in the men of prayer whose petitions have become permanent possessions of the church. They can furnish him with ideas, and help him to keep his public prayers out of a narrow rut of thought and interest. Our Lord's immediate response to his disciples when they came saying, "Teach us to pray" would seem to encourage us to turn for help to any man of prayer who can broaden our understanding of the possibilities before us in this most delicate and important task. Dr. John Kelman said in these lectures [41] long ago that it was his custom just before going into a service of worship to steep himself in the great prayers of others, and so to go to the high office of a priest in the

[41] *The War and Preaching*, p. 162.

mood and spirit into which he was called to lead others. The posthumous publication of some of Dr. Kelman's prayers [42] makes it plain that sometimes at least he wrote his prayers with the utmost care. Whether a prayer be composed in the study prior to its being offered in public, or be composed in the church simultaneously with its being given spoken expression, it can be a worthier offering if the spirit out of which it comes has been nourished and fed by the spirit of prayer which has been the continuing possession of the Church of God.

If public prayers are robbed of reality when enshrined in the archaic language of mediaevalism, it is equally true that they are robbed of their essential universality when expressed in the vocabulary peculiar to a particular group. This is the moral argument against the use of temporarily prevalent colloquialisms in public prayer. It is not that such expressions have not yet been accepted as good English usage. In the light of eternity, that is a small matter. But when the leader of worship attempts to create an atmosphere of reality by introducing into public prayer the catchwords of the day, he achieves several unfortunate results on the human side. He generally makes it obvious that he is trying to create an atmosphere, thereby destroying the very reality he is seeking to discover. He is also pretty sure to push outside the circle of spiritual interest some one to whom that particular catchword has become a weariness of the flesh. Most serious of all, he identifies the prayer with the special group who are under the spell of that verbal novelty. The restrictive influence of such expressions is all the more potent if they constitute the professional vocabulary of a particular vocation,

[42] *Prayers and Meditations*, privately printed.

or if they are commonly flaunted in the face of society as an indication that their user is at home in some esoteric circle of learning. (Even psychologists, philosophers, and theologians sometimes succumb to the temptation of linguistic exhibitionism!) The language of prayer ought to carry intimations of the universal love of God which answers the universal need of man. The ideal language for public prayer would be a universal language. Wanting that, we must use a medley of tongues, and pray that they may be baptized with a Pentecostal universality of spirit. We must not quench that universal spirit under words that exaggerate our differences and obscure the life that all men can find in God.

X

It is because music is such a universal language that it is the ideal medium for expressing some of the moods of worship. I was once walking almost knee-deep in mud through the center of a street in the Chinese city at Harbin when over all the street-cries and hubbub of Oriental life, there came from an upper room near by the music of "Abide with Me." I hunted out the little company of worshippers, but we had no common language through which we could talk to each other. Change and decay were visible all around us, but only though a hymn-tune that we all loved could we pray for the abiding presence of Him who changeth not. The Oxford Conference in 1937 found in St. Mary's Church that it was possible to sing hymns in three languages at the same time, so long as all followed the same music. But it must be admitted that church music has been a divisive as well as a unifying influence. Great advances have been made in the training of organists and choir masters to understand the religious as well as the aesthetic contribution which they are called into the service of the church to render. Not so much has been done in the perhaps more difficult field of training ministers to appreciate the subtle and intimate relationship between music and religion. Still less has been done in the education of congregations to enter into music as a form of worship. This will always be difficult, because there will always be variations in the appreciation and understanding of music, but much can be accomplished by those who have competence and zeal for the task.

In 1880 two young men formed a partnership in the First Presbyterian Church of Brooklyn, the Reverend Charles Cuthbert Hall in the pulpit and Mr. R. Huntington Woodman at the organ. Dr. Hall had lived with Dean Stanley in England, and had been profoundly influenced by the Anglican musical tradition. Mr. Woodman was a student of Dudley Buck, and later of César Franck in Paris. They set out to raise the standard of the music in the church which they served, and insofar as they could in the community. They believed that only the best music has any place in the worship of God who is the Author of beauty. They believed that the cheap sentimentalism which characterized much of the church music of the day was incongruous with the austere worship of the God of truth. They believed that music should not be an appendage to a service of worship, nor an interlude, nor an extraneous ornament, nor bait used to lure people within hearing distance of a sermon, but an integral part of a unified service. They believed that a chorus choir was preferable to a quartet in which individual

personalities were inevitably conspicuous. They believed
that a congregation would respond to the best, if given a
chance. They were right. They worked together for seven-
teen years, and Mr. Woodman has recently completed sixty-
one years of service, carrying on the tradition which they
established together. As one without musical training who
had the privilege for several years of worshipping under Mr.
Woodman's ministry of music, as I now have under that of
Mr. Carl F. Mueller, I can testify that good music is a means
of grace, and that a man who devotes this art to the glory of
God can lead his fellows in and out of the pulpit into holy
places where words fail and the splendor of God is unveiled.
There is an inscription on a grave in the Lady Chapel at
Durham Cathedral which reads:

> "John Brimlies body here doth ly
> Who praysed God with hand and voice
> By musickes heavenlie harmonie
> Dull minds he maid in God rejoice
> His soul into the heavenes is lyft
> To praise Him still that gave the gyft."

Again and again as the church forgets that music is one of the
voices of God, it needs to have someone say to it, "Stir up the
gift that is in thee."

XI

Whether it be music, however, or words, or symbols
through which the human spirit responds to the God who
seeks our worship, the reality of such fellowship with God
must always be tested by its fruits in the life of the worshippers. There is a noble prayer from the fifth century
Liturgy of Malabar:

"Grant, O Lord, that the ears which have heard the voice of thy songs may be closed to the voice of clamour and dispute; that the eyes which have seen thy great love may also behold thy blessed hope; that the tongues which have sung thy praise may speak the truth; that the feet which have walked in thy courts may walk in the region of light; and that the souls of all who have received thy blessed Sacrament may be restored to newness of life." Unless worship does produce such results, it is mere aestheticism. The results may not be immediately apparent, any more than the flowers in a garden may be expected to spring full blown from the soil the day the seed is planted and the sun shines or the rain falls. But where there is a genuine transaction between God and man, there are fruits. The first evidence that there are results is the kind of discontent with the world as it is which becomes an ideal of the world as it ought to be. "Just so far as you can tolerate the injustice, the cruelty, the dirt and degradation that is in the world, just so sure can you be that you have not seen Him," wrote Studdert-Kennedy. "The test and hall mark of the vision is the strength of your rebellion against it." [43] The final evidence that there are results from worship is power to become and to make all things new. In Bunyan's *Pilgrim's Progress*, it was after leaving the Interpreter's House that Christian came to a place where stood a Cross, and the burden which he had carried on his shoulders was loosed and fell from his back into the pit, so that he saw it no more. "Then he stood still awhile to look and wonder; for it was very surprising to him, that the sight of the Cross should thus ease him of his Bur-

[43] *The New Man In Christ*, by G. A. Studdert-Kennedy, p. 224.

den." And there came to him three Shining Ones, who said,
Peace be to thee.

> "Who's this? the Pilgrim. How! 'tis very true,
>   Old things are passed away, all's become new." [44]

XII

Our worship of the living God revealed in Christ is the
pledge of our faith in the future. A man in the English Lake
District recently watched people going to church across the
road from his hotel, and wrote to the editor of *The New
Statesman*: "These people all attend divine service over the
way. What petitions do they offer there? Is it as simple and
pitiable as 'Lord, send us again what we have always been
used to'?" [45] God forbid that our worship should reach
forth to no more noble permanence than that! Christian
worship gives thanks for a Providence visible in the past,
but it is an affirmation of faith in what may be and shall be
because God is. It is even more than aspiration for what
ought to be. As Baron von Hugel said, "No amount of
Oughtnesses can be made to take the place of one Isness." [46]
Christian worship contemplates with reverence and loyalty
the God who is, and so has evidence of things not seen
which are to be.

AE wrote of some Irishmen who lived by faith:

> "We are less children of this clime
>   Than of some nation yet unborn
>   Or empire in the womb of time.
>   We hold the Ireland in the heart

[44] P. 42 in the P. F. Collier & Sons edition.
[45] Issue of November 2, 1940.
[46] *Letters of Baron Friedrich von Hugel*, p. 174.

> More than the land our eyes have seen,
> And love the goal for which we start
> More than the tale of what has been." [47]

So in the midst of war, and of all the social injustices which breed wars and follow wars, setting our hands to all the stern tasks which must be undertaken and carried through to prevent worse wrongs, we lift our eyes to God, the one unshaken Reality in the midst of tottering worlds, whose Word is *really* the last best hope of earth. Through preaching, through ministries of mercy, through its own fellowship, through worship the Christian church brings to this warring world the one Word by which we can live and go confidently forward: "The Word of the Lord endureth for ever. And this is the Word which by the gospel is preached unto you." [48]

[47] Amos P. Wilder, *The Spiritual Aspects of the New Poetry*, p. 22.

[48] I Peter 1:25.

THE LYMAN BEECHER LECTURES ON PREACHING [1]

Yale University Divinity School

Established May 2, 1872 by Mr. Henry W. Sage in honor of Reverend Lyman Beecher, D.D.

1871–1872   Henry Ward Beecher, *Yale Lecturers on Preaching*, first series, N.Y., J. B. Ford & Company, 1872.

1872–1873   Henry Ward Beecher, *Yale Lectures on Preaching*, second series, N.Y., J. B. Ford & Company, 1873.

1873–1874   Henry Ward Beecher, *Yale Lectures on Preaching*, third series, N.Y., J. B. Ford & Company, 1874. A one volume edition, *Yale Lectures on Preaching*, published by The Pilgrim Press, Chicago.

1874–1875   John Hall, *God's Word Through Preaching*, N.Y., Dodd & Mead, 1875.

1875–1876   William Mackergo Taylor, *The Ministry of the Word*. N.Y., Anson D. F. Randolph & Co., 1876.

1876–1877   Phillips Brooks, *Lectures on Preaching*. N.Y., E. P. Dutton, 1877.

1877–1878   Robert William Dale, *Nine Lectures on Preaching*. N.Y., A. S. Barnes & Co., 1878.

1878–1879   Matthew Simpson, *Lectures on Preaching*. N.Y., Nelson & Phillips, 1879.

1879–1880   Howard Crosby, *The Christian Preacher*. N.Y., Anson D. F. Randolph & Co., 1880.

1880–1881   Joseph Tuthill Duryea, George Harris, Samuel E. Herrick, Nathaniel Judson Burton, and Llewelyn David Bevan. Lectures not published.

1881–1882   Ezekiel Gilman Robinson, *Lectures on Preaching*. N.Y., Henry Holt & Company, Inc., 1883.

1882–1883   No lectures.

[1] Compiled by Reverend Hal Earl Norton, D.D., Pastor, The Roundy Memorial Baptist Church, Milwaukee, Wisconsin.

1883–1884   Nathaniel Judson Burton, *Yale Lectures on Preaching and Other Writings*. Pilgrim Press, 1887. Reprinted by Macmillan Company, 1925, under title of *In Pulpit and Parish*.

1884–1885   Henry Martin Storrs, *The American Preacher*. Not published.

1885–1886   William Mackergo Taylor, *The Scottish Pulpit*. N.Y., Harper & Brothers, 1887.

1886–1887   Washington Gladden, *Tools and the Man*. Boston, Houghton Mifflin Company, 1893.

1887–1888   Henry Clay Trumbull, *The Sunday School*. Philadelphia, John P. Wattles, 1888.

1888–1889   John Albert Broadus, *Preparation and Delivery of Sermons*. N.Y., Harper & Brothers, 1897.

1889–1890   Adolphus Julius Frederick Behrends, *The Philosophy of Preaching*. N.Y., Charles Scribner's Sons, 1893.

1890–1891   James Stalker, *The Preacher and His Models*. N.Y., A. C. Armstrong, 1893.

1891–1892   Andrew Martin Fairbairn, *The Place of Christ in Modern Theology*. N.Y., Charles Scribner's Sons, 1893.

1892–1893   Robert Foreman Horton, *Verbum Dei*. N.Y., Macmillan Company, 1893.

1893–1894   No lectures.

1894–1895   David Hummell Greer, *The Preacher and His Place*. N.Y., Charles Scribner's Sons, 1895.

1895–1896   Henry van Dyke, *The Gospel for an Age of Doubt*, N.Y., Macmillan Company, 1896.

1896–1897   John Watson (Ian Maclaren), *The Cure of Souls*. N.Y., Dodd & Mead, 1896.

1897–1898   William Jewett Tucker, *The Making and the Unmaking of the Preacher*. Boston, Houghton Mifflin Company, 1898.

1898–1899   Sir George Adam Smith, *Modern Criticism and the Preaching of the Old Testament*. N.Y., A. C. Armstrong, 1901.

1899–1900   John Brown, *Puritan Preaching in England*. N.Y., Charles Scribner's Sons, 1900.

1900–1901   No lectures.

1901–1902   Washington Gladden, *Social Salvation*. Boston, Houghton Mifflin Company, 1902.

1902–1903   George Angier Gordon, *Ultimate Conceptions of Faith*. Boston, Houghton Mifflin Company, 1903.

1903–1904   Lyman Abbott, *The Christian Ministry*. Boston, Houghton Mifflin Company, 1905.

1904–1905   Francis Greenwood Peabody, *Jesus Christ and the Christian Character*. N.Y., Macmillan Company, 1908.

1905–1906   Charles Reynolds Brown, *The Social Message of the Modern Pulpit*. N.Y., Charles Scribner's Sons, 1906.

1906–1907   Peter Taylor Forsyth, *Positive Preaching and the Modern Mind*. London, Hodder & Stoughton, 1907.

1907–1908   William Herbert Perry Faunce, *The Educational Ideal in the Ministry*. N.Y., Macmillan Company, 1908; reprinted 1919.

1908–1909   Herbert Hensley Hensen, *The Liberty of Prophesying*. New Haven, Yale University Press, 1910.

1909–1910   Charles Edward Jefferson, *The Building of the Church*. N.Y., Macmillan Company, 1910.

1910–1911   Frank Wakeley Gunsaulus, *The Minister and the Spiritual Life*. N.Y., Fleming H. Revell, 1911.

1911–1912   John Henry Jowett, *The Preacher: His Life and Work*. N.Y., George H. Doran, 1912.

1912–1913   Charles Henry Parkhurst, *The Pulpit and the Pew*. New Haven, Yale University Press, 1913.

1913–1914   Charles Sylvester Horne, *The Romance of Preaching*. N.Y., Fleming H. Revell, 1914.

1914–1915 George Wharton Pepper, *A Voice from the Crowd*. New Haven, Yale University Press, 1915.

1915–1916 William DeWitt Hyde, *The Gospel of Good Will*. N.Y., Macmillan Company, 1916.

1916–1917 William Fraser McDowell, *Good Ministers of Jesus Christ*. N.Y., Abingdon Press, 1917.

1917–1918 Henry Sloane Coffin, *In a Day of Social Rebuilding*. New Haven, Yale University Press, 1918.

1918–1919 John Kelman, *The War and Preaching*. New Haven, Yale University Press, 1919.

1919–1920 Albert Parker Fitch, *Preaching and Paganism*. New Haven, Yale University Press, 1920.

1920–1921 Charles David Williams, *The Prophetic Ministry for Today*. N.Y., Macmillan Company, 1921.

1921–1922 William Pierson Merrill, *The Freedom of the Preacher*, N.Y., Macmillan Company, 1922.

1922–1923 Charles Reynolds Brown, *The Art of Preaching*. N.Y., Macmillan Company, 1922.

1923–1924 Harry Emerson Fosdick, *The Modern Use of the Bible*. N.Y., Macmillan Company, 1924.

1924–1925 William Ralph Inge, *The Preaching of the Kingdom of God in History*. Lectures not published.

1925–1926 Raymond Calkins, *The Eloquence of the Christian Experience*. N.Y., Macmillan Company, 1927.

1926–1927 John Robert Paterson Sclater, *The Public Worship of God*. N.Y., Doubleday, Doran, 1927.

1927–1928 James Edward Freeman, *The Ambassador*. N.Y., Macmillan Company, 1928.

1928–1929 Edwin Du Bose Mouzon, *Preaching with Authority*. N.Y., Macmillan Company, 1929.

1929–1930 Francis John McConnell, *The Prophetic Ministry*. N.Y., Abingdon Press, 1930.

1930–1931 George Arthur Buttrick, *Jesus Came Preaching*. N.Y., Charles Scribner's Sons, 1931.

1931–1932 Ernest Fremont Tittle, *Jesus After Nineteen Centuries*. N.Y., Abingdon Press, 1932.

1932–1933   Lawrence Pearsall Jacks, *Elemental Religion*. N.Y.,
            Harper & Brothers, 1934.

1933–1934   Albert Edward Day, *Jesus and Human Personality*.
            N.Y., Abingdon Press, 1934.

1934–1935   Walter Russell Bowie, *The Renewing Gospel*. N.Y.,
            Charles Scribner's Sons, 1935.

1935–1936   John Edgar Park, *The Miracle of Preaching*. N.Y.,
            Macmillan Company, 1936.

1936–1937   No lectures.

1937–1938   Willard Learoyd Sperry, *We Prophesy in Part*. N.Y.,
            Harper & Brothers, 1938.

1938–1939   Charles Clayton Morrison, *What Is Christianity?*
            Chicago, Willett, Clark & Company, 1940.

1939–1940   George Arthur Buttrick, Edwin McNeill Poteat,
            Arthur Howe Bradford, Elmore McNeill McKee,
            Wyatt Aiken Smart, and Ernest Fremont Tittle,
            Preaching in These Times. N.Y., Charles Scribner's
            Sons, 1940.

1940–1941   Ralph Washington Sockman, *The Highway of God*.
            N.Y., Macmillan Company, 1942.

INDEX

Acquisitiveness, 187
Activism, 84, 192
Acts, Book of, 135, 173, 192
Administrator, 150-151
Adult Education, 162
Adventures of Ideas, 38
AE, 207
Avignon, 195
Allen, A. V. G., 106, 183
Altar, 197
Ambition, 26-27
Amen, Harlan P., 132
Andrewes, Lancelot, 201
Angelo, Michael, 121
Apostolic age, 21
Art, 179, 195
Art of Preaching, The, 23
Atlantic Monthly, The, 101, 159, 184
Augustine, 113
Authority, 23, 25-26, 28, 138-139
Auto-suggestion, 119-120, 185

Background, 95
Bacon, Leonard, 161
Ballots, 74
Barbour, G. F., 59
Barnett, Samuel, 146-147
Barry, F. R., 43, 64-65, 115
Barthian Theology, 14
Basic Convictions, 174, 177
Baxter, Richard, 29, 167
Beauty, 180, 187, 204
Beecher, Lyman, 159
Beliefs, 59
Bellamy, Joseph, 25
Benét, William Rose, 85-86
Bergson, Henri, 182
Bible, 8-15, 121, 137, 163, 179, 183
Bible in Spain, 186
Bible Society, 84-85
Bishop, Abraham, 78
Borrow, George, 186
Boswell, James, 46-47
Bowers, Claude G., 78
Bradford, Gamaliel, 5
Breshkovskaya, Catharine, 57

British Army, 159
British Weekly, 110, 189
Brooks, Van Wyck, 151
Brooks, Phillips, 106, 183
Brothers Karamazov, 58, 107
Brown, John, 97
Browning, Robert, 190
Buck, Dudley, 204
Bunyan, John, 206
Burning Bush, 41, 119-120

Cabot, Richard C., 182
Canby, Henry S., 117, 194
Canon Law, 23
Cardozo, Benjamin, 194
Carlyle, Thomas, 100, 127
Cathedral Church of St. Paul, 130
Central Bureau for Relief, 48
Chain of Prayer Across the Ages, A., 201
Chaplin, Maxwell, 65
Chase, Mary Ellen, 123
Chesterton, G. K., 75-76, 132, 188-189
Christian Century, The, 194
Christian News-Letter, 56, 159
Christian Social Union, 76
Church, 20-22, 35-66, 69, 86, 93-101, 111-112, 155-158, 168, 169, 179
Church and its Function in Society, The, 48
Church of Scotland, 65
Civilization, 70, 121, 160, 186
Clap, Thomas, 161
Class consciousness, 57-58
Clough, Arthur Hugh, 184
Cole, G. D. H., 56
Colossians, Epistle to, 33
Communion, 184, 199
Community, 35, 54, 69, 98, 151-154, 169
Compassion, 96-7
Compromise, 75, 114-116
Concerning the Ministry, 137
Confessional, 148
Confessions of an Opium Eater, 28
Conscience, 73, 79, 86, 115, 177

215

Cooperation, 157
Corinthians, First Epistle to, 79
Counsellor, 143-149
Cox, Donald, 183
Creativity, 182
Creatures, 189, 190
Cross, 128-130, 195, 197, 206

Dante, 121
De Quincey, Thomas, 28-29
Dearmer, Percy, 179
Death, 123
Dedication, 181, 194-195
Decisions, 164
Democracy, 56, 80, 106, 110, 113
Denney, James, 143
Denominations, 50-52, 155-158
Devotion, 201-202
Director of Religious Education, 162
Discontent, 206
D'Orge, Jeanne, 149
Dormi Secure, 7
Dostoievski, Feodor, 58, 107
Durham Cathedral, 205
Dynamic, 184

Ecumenical Church, 46-52, 99-100
Education, 158-166
Edwards, Jonathan, 30, 109
Eliot, Charles W., 7, 152
Eliot, George, 176
Eliot, T. S., 101
Elliott, Phillips P., 54
Embezzled Heaven, 107-8
Emerson, Ralph Waldo, 84, 141, 158, 181
Emotion, 176, 185, 193
Ends and Means, 90
Erskine, John, 165-166
Essay on Going to Church, An, 40
Ethical Instruction in Schools, 146
Exupèry, Antoine de Saint, 184
Ezekiel, 1

Failure, 71-72
Faith, 93, 108, 119, 133, 207
Faith in Dark Ages, 115
Fatalism, 125
Federal Council Bulletin, 100
Fellowship, 94, 95, 112
Finding God, 185
Fine Gold of Newman, 38
Flight to Arras, 184
Force, 91

Forgiveness, 13-15, 113-14, 128
Fox, Selina F., 201
Francis, St., 132
Franck, César, 204
Fredericksburg, 99
Freedom, 31, 38, 75, 76, 78-79, 83, 91, 92, 182
Friends, Society of, 75, 175, 196
Friendship, 140-143
Froude, J. A., 127
Frustration, 108, 131, 163
Furness, Horace H., 98-99

Generosity, 92
Geneva, 47
Gladden, Washington, 81, 166
Glover, T. R., 141
Gordon, George A., 25
Gore, Charles, 43
Grace, 28, 128, 168, 196, 199
Gray, Herbert, 185
Groups, 79-80
Guidance, 4, 128
Guild of St. Matthew, 175

Habits, 163, 182
Hadfield, J. A., 119
Hadley, Arthur T., 189
Hall, Charles Cuthbert, 204-205
Harbin, 203
Hardman, Oscar, 7
Hatred, 92, 95
Havergal, Frances R., 195
Hendrick, Burton J., 98
Henson, Hensley, 77-8
Herod, 87-88
Hibbert Journal, 37, 41
Higher Pantheism, The, 192
History of Christian Worship, 7
History of the Expansion of Christianity, 55
Hocking, William E., 182, 192
Home Prayers, 200
Homes, 163, 169
Hope, 30-31, 48
Hounds of Spring, 109
Humanism in New England Theology, 25
Humanity, 130, 132
Hutton, John A., 189
Hwai Yuen, 65

Ideologists, To., 86
Imagination, 177, 195

Imitation of Christ, 200
Immanence, 12-13, 189
Individual, 86, 105-107
Industrialism, 119
Influence, 147
Inge, W. R., 123-4, 158
Initiative, Divine, 185-186
Inspiration, 4, 5
Interest, 9-10, 167-168
International Agencies, 91, 97-98
Interpreter, The, 149
Intuition, 4
Isaiah, 188, 191

Jacks, L. P., 120
James, Henry, 112
James, Henry, Jr., 7
James, William, 111, 119, 183, 195
Japan, 100
Jefferson, and Hamilton, 78
Jeremiah, 138
Jesus Christ, 15-20, 36, 39, 41, 64-65, 70, 87, 89-90, 110-111, 114-115, 117, 124, 128, 130-133, 166, 168-169, 191, 192, 195, 196, 201
Jesus of History, The, 142
Jewish Institute of Religion, 194
Joad, C. E. M., 72
John, First Epistle of, 39
John, Gospel of, 87
Johnson, Samuel, 46-47
Journal of a Tour to the Hebrides, 47
Jowett, Benjamin, 146
Jowett, John H., 168
Judgment, 30, 87-88
Justin Martyr, 73

Kelman, John, 201-202
Kempis, Thomas à, 200
Kingdom of God, 42, 69-70, 98, 115

Language, 202-3
Laodiceans, 123
Latourette, Kenneth S., 55
Law, 91
Law, William, 26-27
Leadership, 138-139
Leber, Charles T., 54
Legalism, 17-18, 89
Lepers, 63
Life and I, 6
Life and Work, 66
Lincoln, Abraham, 81, 99
Lippmann, Walter, 121

Liturgy, 174, 175, 198
Liturgy of Malabar, 205-206
Liu, Timothy T., 96
London, 65, 168
Love, 90, 167
Luke, Gospel of, 67
Lutherans, 138

MacDonald, Ramsay, 111
Machinery, 38, 118, 187
Magic, 124-125
Mansfield, Katherine, 126-7
Marius the Epicurean, 194, 195
Martineau, James, 200
Martyn, Henry, Life of, 58
Masefield, John, 5
Matthew, Gospel of, 66, 67, 87
McAfee, Mildred, 159
McConnachie, John, 14
McKenzie, John G., 183
Meaning, 107, 118, 166, 188
Meaning of God in Human Experience, 182, 192
Methods of Private Religious Living, 119
Migrants, 63
Mill, J. S., 96
Milton, John, 131
Miniver, Mrs., 44
Missions, 52-55, 174
Mistral, Frederic, 118
Modes of Thought, 26
Montague, Margaret Prescott, 184
Morley, John, 96
Mueller, Carl F., 205
Music, 203-205
Murry, J. Middleton, 126
Mystics, 182, 193

Near East Relief, 63
New England Indian Summer, 151
New Man in Christ, The, 206
New Statesman, 72, 207
New Testament, 37
Newman, John Henry, 38
Noyes, Joseph, 161

Oldham, J. H., 48, 78-79, 159
Oman, John, 137
On Journey, 58
Open Conspiracy, The, 59
Orchard, William E., 180, 190
Organists, 204-205
Organization, 63, 97, 150-151
Outspoken Essays, 158

Owst, G. R., 77
Oxford Conference, 47, 49, 82, 203
Oxford Movement, 40-1

Pacifism, 88-92
Padwyck, Constance, 58
Page, Walter H., 97-8
Palmer, George Herbert, 146
Pastor, 23-24, 129, 137-169
Pater, Walter, 194, 195
Patrick, Simon, 29
Paul, St., 79, 84, 192
Peace-making, 92
Penitence, 92
Pentecost, 173
Perfectionism, 19
Perry, Bliss, 85
Perry, Ralph Barton, 195
Personal Problems in Conduct and Religion, 183
Personal Religion and the Life of Devotion, 124
Personality, 120, 121, 191-192
Perspective, 94-95, 183
Peter, First Epistle of, 102, 208
Petre, M. D., 127, 168
Pharisees, 87
Phillips Exeter Academy, 132
Philosophy, 26
Pike, James S., 100
Pilgrim's Progress, 206
Pilgrim's Way, 28
Plato, 121
Plain Talk, 39
Plebiscites, 73
Pliny, 173
Poetry, 5
Police, 90-91
Politics, 78
Portrait of a Lady, 112
Possessions, 118
Prayer, 93, 119, 130, 173, 175, 180, 189-192
Prayers and Meditations, 202
Preces Privatae, 201
Preface to Morals, 121
Presbyterian, 46-47, 75
Problem, The, 181
Promotion, 155-156, 166
Propaganda, 164-166
Protestantism, 73-74
Psalms, Book of, 188
Psychiatry, 108, 145, 154
Psychology, 119, 167

Psychology and Morals, 119
Punishment, 123-124
Purpose, 118, 177

Rab and His Friends, 97
Rainsford, W. S., 64
Rauschenbusch, Walter, 83
Real Estate, 57
Receptivity, 192-193
Reformers, 21
Reilly, J. J., 38
Release, 183
Religion in the Making, 40
Religious Experience and Scientific Method, 182
Religious Perplexities, 120
Renaissance in Italy, 121
Renan, Ernest, 195
Representative Government, 73
Research, 165
Resolutions, 73
Response, 177, 185, 187
Relevance of the Church, The, 43
Revelation, 14
Revelation, Book of, 123, 171
Rhythm, 201
Ritter, Charles, 195
Robinson, John, 21
Rock, The, 101
Rogers, George B., 132
Romola, 176
Roosevelt, Theodore, 118
Rural regions, 186-187

Sacrament, 206
Sacrifice, 195, 197
St. Columba, 65
St. George's Church, 64
St. Mary's Church, 49
Saints, 22, 37, 43, 120
Salvation, 28, 69, 166
Saturday Review of Literature, The, 86, 117, 166
Savonarola, 121
Scott, Walter, 167
Scribes, 23
Scribner's Magazine, 119
Scudder, Doremus, 53
Scudder, Vida, 57
Selected English Sermons, 77
Self-consciousness, 137-138
Self-sufficiency, 186
Serious Call to a Devout and Holy Life, 27

Shaw, George Bernard, 39-40
Shepherd, 138, 143
Simeon, Charles, 58
Simplicity, 196
Sin, 70, 189, 190, 191
Sincerity, 175, 181, 199
Slavery, 38, 81, 85
Smith, Frederick, 122
Smyth, Charles, 23
Snows of Helicon, 3
Social Agencies, 61-63, 145, 153-154
Social Ethics, 71-85, 175
Söderblom, Archbishop, 117
Solidarity, 184
Solitariness, 40
Sorrow, 121-131
Soul, 119, 142, 167
Spectator, 179
Spiritual Aspects of the New Poetry, The, 208
Spiritual Life, The, 193
Spontaneity, 180
Stanley, Arthur P., 204
Statistical method, 159
Stein, Alexis, 131
Stewart, George, 65
Stoics, 125
Story of a Varied Life, The, 64
Struther, Jan, 45
Studdert-Kennedy, G. A., 206
Students, 109, 160
Suffering, 96-97, 121-131
Superstition, 124-125
Sursum Corda, 198
Symbols, 196-198
Symonds, John Addington, 121

Tchertkoff, Vladimir, 167
Teacher, 158-166
Temple, William, 174, 177
Tennyson, Alfred, 192
Things That Matter Most, 168
Thompson, Sylvia, 109
Thoreau, Henry, 24, 193-4
Time, 44
Toc H., 183
Tolstoy, Leo, 115, 167
Tomlinson, H. M., 3
Toynbee Hall, 146
Tradition, 45, 159, 163
Transcendence, 13-14
Truth, 7, 167, 187, 204
Tweedsmuir, Lord, 27-28, 167

Two Sources of Morality and Religion, The, 182
Tyrrell, George, 127, 168, 189

Underhill, Evelyn, 37, 40, 177, 192
Undset, Sigrid, 41, 119
Unity, Church, 49-52, 156-158

Van Waters, Miriam, 111
Varieties of Religious Experience, The, 119
Variety, 57, 95, 179
Visitation, 147-148
Visser 't Hooft, W. A., 48
Vitality, 193-194
von Hugel, Friedrich, 125, 137, 189, 207

Walden Pond, 193-4
War, 75, 85-100, 160, 208
War and Preaching, The, 201
Way of Simplicity, The, 180, 190
Webb, Clement, 189
Wellesley College, 159
Wells, H. G., 59
Werden, John of, 7
Werfel, Franz, 107
What Men Live By, 182
Where Lies the Land, 184
White, Andrew D., 115
Whitefield, George, 30
Whitehead, Alfred N., 26, 38, 40
Wholeness, 182
Whyte, Alexander, 59, 167
Wieman, Henry N., 119, 182
Wilder, Amos P., 208
Will, 164, 176, 177, 192, 194, 195
Will to Go, The, 184
Wilson, Woodrow, 97
Windswept, 123
Winslow, Ola E., 30, 109
With Francis Furini, 190
Woodman, R. Huntington, 204-205
World, 69-101
World Council of Churches, 48
World Student Christian Federation, 49
Work, 59-64, 187
Worship, 39-41, 49, 60, 118, 173-208
Worship, 177
Wright, Henry B., 160, 161

Yale Review, The, 194
Yale University, 105, 159-160, 161
Youth, 108-112, 159-166
Youth in Conflict, 111